AAT

Foundation Certificate in Accounting
Foundation Diploma in Accounting
Synoptic Assessment

Pocket Notes

These Pocket Notes support study for the following AAT qualifications:

AAT Foundation Certificate in Accounting – Level 2

AAT Foundation Diploma in Accounting and Business – Level 2

AAT Foundation Certificate in Bookkeeping – Level 2

AAT Foundation Award in Accounting Software – Level 2

AAT Level 2 Award in Accounting Skills to Run Your Business

AAT Foundation Certificate in Accounting at SCQF Level 5

KAPLAN PUBLISHING

British library cataloguing-in-publication data

A catalogue record for this book is available from the British Library.

Published by:
Kaplan Publishing UK
Unit 2 The Business Centre
Molly Millars Lane
Wokingham
Berkshire
RG41 2QZ

ISBN 978-1-78740-542-4

© Kaplan Financial Limited, 2019

Printed and bound in Great Britain.

CONTENTS

Page Number

A guide to the assessment 1

Bookkeeping Transactions

Chapter 1	Books of prime entry 7
Chapter 2	Double entry bookkeeping – an introduction.. 23
Chapter 3	Ledger accounting.. 29
Chapter 4	Accounting for credit sales, VAT and discounts...................................... 41
Chapter 5	Accounting for credit purchases, VAT and discounts 45
Chapter 6	Control accounts and subsidiary ledgers 49
Chapter 7	Receipts and payments.. 65

Bookkeeping Controls

Chapter 8	Errors and suspense accounts... 89
Chapter 9	Control account reconciliations 101
Chapter 10	Payroll procedures 123
Chapter 11	Bank reconciliations 131

Elements of Costing

Chapter 12 Materials and inventory 139

Chapter 13 Labour costs 145

Chapter 14 Budgeting 149

Work Effectively in Finance

Chapter 15 The role of the finance function 153

Chapter 16 Comparison and communication of information 159

Chapter 17 Planning and organising work 165

Chapter 18 Working relationships 171

Chapter 19 Policies, procedures and legislation 179

Chapter 20 Improving your own performance 185

Chapter 21 Ethics and sustainability 189

Index I.1

Preface

These Pocket Notes contain the key things that you need to know for the exam, presented in a unique visual way that makes revision easy and effective.

Written by experienced lecturers and authors, these Pocket Notes break down content into manageable chunks to maximise your concentration.

Quality and accuracy are of the utmost importance to us so if you spot an error in any of our products, please send an email to mykaplanreporting@kaplan.com with full details, or follow the link to the feedback form in MyKaplan.

Our Quality Co-ordinator will work with our technical team to verify the error and take action to ensure it is corrected in future editions.

A guide to the assessment

The assessment

The synoptic assessment is a compulsory component of the AAT Foundation Certificate and Foundation Diploma qualification. It combines elements of learning outcomes from the following units into a scenario-based assessment:

- Bookkeeping Transactions
- Bookkeeping Controls
- Elements of Costing
- Work Effectively in Finance

Not all of the learning outcomes of the above units is assessable in the synoptic assessment.

Based upon the specimen assessments released by AAT, the synoptic assessment will comprise seven tasks, based upon a 'scenario', and will be for two hours. The synoptic assessment is partially human-marked and partially computer-marked.

Pass mark

To pass an assessment, students need to achieve a mark of 70% or more.

Scope of content

The syllabus for the synoptic assessment comprises four Assessment Objectives based upon the learning objectives of the underlying units as follows:

Assessment Objective	Weighting
A01	24%
Demonstrate an understanding of the finance function and the roles and procedures carried out by members of an accounting team	
A02	24%
Process transactions, complete calculations and make journal entries	
A03	34%
Compare, produce and reconcile journals and accounts	
A04	18%
Communicate financial information effectively	
Total	**100%**

Composition of assessment objectives

Assessment objective 1	Demonstrate an understanding of the finance function and the roles and procedures carried out by members of an accounting team
Related learning outcomes	**Work Effectively in Finance** LO1 Understand the finance function within an organisation LO2 Use personal skills development in finance LO3 Produce work effectively LO4 Understand Corporate Social Responsibility (CSR), ethics and sustainability within organisations
Assessment objective 2	Process transactions, complete calculations and make journal entries
Related learning outcomes	**Bookkeeping Transactions** LO2 Process customer transactions LO3 Process supplier transactions LO4 Process receipts and payments LO5 Process transactions through the ledgers to the trial balance

Assessment objective 3	Compare, produce and reconcile journals and accounts
Related learning outcomes	**Bookkeeping Controls** LO3 Use control accounts LO4 Use the journal LO5 Reconcile a bank statement with the cash book **Elements of Costing** LO2 Use cost recording techniques LO3 Provide information on actual and budgeted costs and income
Assessment objective 4	Communicate financial information effectively
Related learning outcome	**Work Effectively in Finance** LO3 Produce work effectively

1

Books of prime entry

- Introduction.
- Sales day book.
- Sales returns day book.
- Purchases day book.
- Purchases returns day book.
- Cash receipts book.
- VAT.
- Cash payments book.
- Discounts allowed day book.
- Discounts received day book.
- Petty cash book.

Introduction

Rather than entering each individual transaction into the ledger accounts as they happen, books o
prime entry are used to record transactions/documents of the same type before they are processe
further.

Purchases day book purchase invoices	**Purchases returns day book** credit notes from suppliers	**Sales day book** sales invoices	**Sales returns day book** credit notes sent to customers
Petty cash book small cash payments made	**Books of prime entry**		**Cash payments book** cheques/other payments made
Journal adjustments/errors	**Discounts allowed day book** discount allowed to customers	**Discounts received day book** discount received from suppliers	**Cash receipts book** cheques/cash received

Sales day book

- list of invoices sent out to credit customers
- date
- invoice number
- customer name/account code
- invoice total analysed into net, VAT and gross (total)

- information copied from sales invoices
- before further processing, must be totalled
- totals can be checked by cross casting £3,794.14 + £758.82 = £4,552.96.

Sales Day book						
Date	Invoice No	Customer Name	Sales ledger code	Total (gross) £	VAT (20%) £	Net £
12/08/X3	69489	TJ Builder	SL21	2,004.12	334.02	1,670.10
12/08/X3	69490	McCarthy & Sons	SL08	1,485.74	247.62	1,238.12
12/08/X3	69491	Trevor Partner	SL10	1,063.10	177.18	885.92
				4,552.96	758.82	3,794.14

Analysed sales day book

Sometimes the net figure (actual sales) is analysed into different types of sale/product type.

Sales day book

Date	Invoice No	Customer Name	Code	Total (gross) £	VAT £	Russia £	Poland £	Spain £	Germany £	France £
15/08/X1	167	Worldwide News	W5	3,000.00	500.00					2,500.00
	168	Local News	L1	240.00	40.00			200.00		
	169	The Press Today	P2	360.00	60.00				300.00	
	170	Home Call	H1	240.00	40.00			200.00		
	171	Tomorrow	T1	120.00	20.00					100.00
	172	Worldwide news	W5	3,600.00	600.00	3,000.00	–			
				7,560.00	1,260.00	3,000.00	–	400.00	300.00	2,600.00

Sales returns day book

- list of credit notes sent out to credit customers
- date
- credit note number
- customer name/account code
- credit note total analysed into net, VAT and total
- information copied from credit note.

SALES RETURNS DAY BOOK						
Date	Credit Note No.	Customer Name	Code	Total (gross) £	VAT £	Net £
28/08/X3	03561	Trevor Partner	SL10	125.48	20.91	104.57
28/08/X3	03562	TJ Builder	SL21	151.74	25.29	126.45
				277.22	46.20	231.02

Purchases day book

- list of invoices received from credit suppliers
- date
- purchase invoice number (often internal consecutive number allocated)
- supplier name/account code

- invoice total analysed into net, VAT and total (gross)
- information copied from purchase invoice
- before further processing, must be totalled
- totals can be checked by cross casting £663.90 + £132.77 = £796.67.

PURCHASES DAY BOOK						
Date	Invoice No.	code	supplier	Total (gross) £	VAT £	Net £
20X1						
7 May	2814	PL06	J Taylor	190.41	31.73	158.68
8 May	2815	PL13	McMinn Partners	288.14	48.02	240.12
	2816	PL27	D B Bros	96.54	16.09	80.45
9 May	2817	PL03	J S Ltd	221.58	36.93	184.65
				796.67	132.77	663.90

Analysed purchases day book

Sometimes the net figure (actual purchases) is analysed into different types of purchase/product type.

PURCHASES DAY BOOK									
Date	Invoice no	Code	Supplier	Total (gross) £	VAT £	01 £	02 £	03 £	04 £
05/02/X5	1161	053	Calderwood & Co	20.16	3.36	16.80			
05/02/X5	1162	259	Mellor & Cross	112.86	18.81		94.05		
05/02/X5	1163	360	Thompson Bros Ltd	42.86	7.14	35.72			

Purchases returns day book

- list of credit notes received from credit suppliers
- date
- credit note number (often internal consecutive number allocated)
- customer name/account code
- credit note total analysed into net, VAT and total
- information copied from credit note.

PURCHASES RETURNS DAY BOOK						
Date	**Credit note no**	**Supplier**	**Code**	**Total (gross) £**	**VAT £**	**Net £**
09/05/X1	02456	McMinn Partners	PL13	64.80	10.80	54.00
09/05/X1	02457	J S Ltd	PL03	72.00	12.00	60.00
				136.80	22.80	114.00

Cash receipts book

The cash receipts book records all money received into the business bank account for whatever reason.

Cash receipts book

Date	Narrative	Total £	VAT £	Receivables £	Cash sales £	Sundry £
3 Jul	A Brown	20.54	3.42		17.12	
5 Jul	S Smith & Co Ltd	9.30		9.30		
	P Priest	60.80		60.80		
	James & Jeans	39.02	6.50		32.52	
	LS Moore	17.00		17.00		
6 Jul	L White Ltd	5.16		5.16		
7 Jul	M N Furnishers Ltd	112.58				112.58
	R B Roberts	23.65		23.65		
	Light and Shade	86.95		86.95		
		375.00	9.92	202.86	49.64	112.58

| Date of receipt | Details of receipt | Total of receipts | Total VAT on cash sales | Total receipts from receivables | Total receipt for cash sales | Total receipts from sundry income |

- entries to the cash receipts book come from either the remittance list or a photocopy of the paying in slip
- to check the totalling the cross casts should be checked:

	£
VAT	9.92
Receivables	202.86
Cash sales	49.64
Sundry income	112.58
Total	375.00

VAT

- VAT is only ever recorded in the cash receipts book on cash sales or other income
- any VAT on sales on credit (i.e. receipts from receivables) has already been recorded in the sales day book and posted to the ledger accounts from there

Cash payments book

The cash payments book records all money paid out of the business bank account for whatever reason.

Date	Details	Cheque No	Total	VAT	Purchases ledger £	Cash	Post
14/2	K Ellis	1152	80.00		80.00		
15/2	Hutt Ltd	1153	120.00	20.00		100.00	
16/2	Biggs Ltd	1154	200.00				200.00
			400.00	20.00	80.00	100.00	200.00

Date of payment	Details of payment	Total of payment	Total VAT on cash purchases	Total payment to payables	Total payment for cash purchases	Total payment for post

- entries to the cash payments book come from either the cheque stubs or other banking documentation (see later chapter)
- to check the totalling the cross casts should be checked:

	£
VAT	20.00
Purchases ledger	80.00
Cash purchases	100.00
Post	200.00
Total	400.00

VAT is only ever recorded in the cash payments book on cash purchases, or other payments for expenditure that attract VAT, which have not been entered in the purchases day book.

- any VAT on purchases on credit (i.e. payments to payables) has already been recorded in the purchases day book and posted to the ledger accounts from there

Discounts allowed day book

Discounts Allowed Day Book					
Date	Narrative	Reference	Total £	VAT £	Net £
Totals					

Total deduction required to receivables balance

VAT reduction from original VAT amount

Amount of discount allowed expense

The discounts allowed day book records the credit notes issued due to a customer taking advantage of a prompt payment discount.

Discounts received day book

Discounts received day book					
Date	Narrative	Reference	Total £	VAT £	Net £
Totals					

Total deduction required to payables balance

VAT reduction from original VAT amount

Amount of discount received income

The discounts received day book records the credit notes received from a supplier due to us taking advantage of a prompt payment discount.

Petty cash book

- book of prime entry
- often part of general ledger as well
- small cash receipts side
- larger analysed cash payments side.

Receipts side – only one column as only entry is regular payment in cash from bank

Payments side – analysed according to typical expenditure plus VAT column

Imprest amount of £150 to start week

Date of claim

Details

Sequential petty cash voucher number

Analysed payments – total column includes VAT but analysis column amount is net of VAT

PETTY CASH BOOK

RECEIPTS			PAYMENTS								
Date	Narrative	Total £	Date	Narrative	Voucher no	Total £	Postage £	Cleaning £	Tea & Coffee £	Sundry £	VAT £
1 Nov	Bal b/f	35.50									
1 Nov	Cheque	114.50	1 Nov	ASDA	58	23.50			23.50		
			2 Nov	Post Office Ltd	59	29.50	29.50				
			2 Nov	Cleaning materials	60	15.07		12.56			2.51
			3 Nov	Postage	61	16.19	16.19				
			3 Nov	ASDA	62	10.57		8.81			1.76
			4 Nov	Newspapers	63	18.90				18.90	
			5 Nov	ASDA	64	12.10				10.09	2.01
						125.83	45.69	21.37	23.50	28.99	6.28

When petty cash book has been written up for a period it must be totalled. Totals should then be checked by cross-casting:

	£
Postage	45.69
Cleaning	21.37
Tea & coffee	23.50
Sundry	28.99
VAT	6.28
Total	125.83

2

Double entry bookkeeping – an introduction

- Principles of double entry bookkeeping.
- The accounting equation.
- Types of income and expense.

Principles of double entry bookkeeping

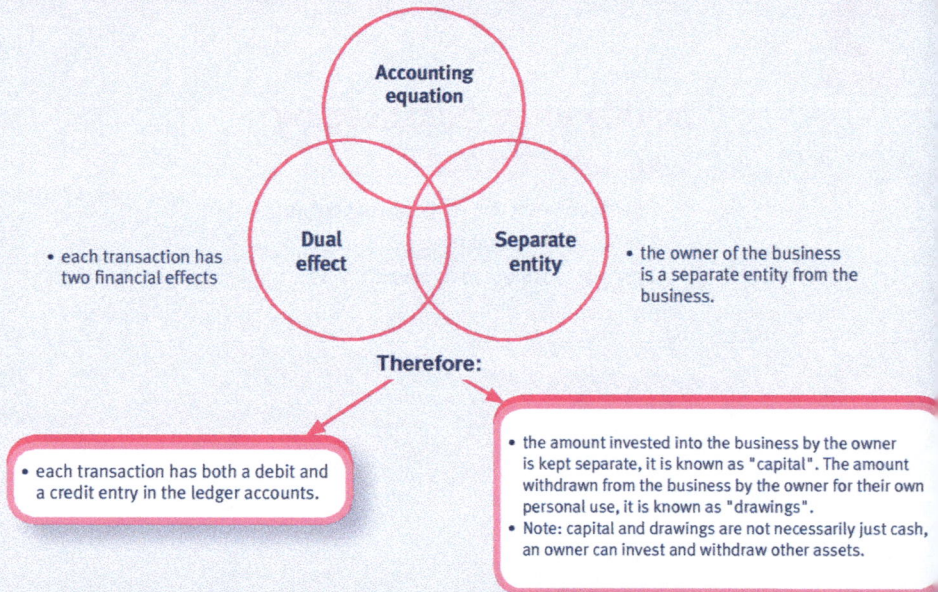

- each transaction has two financial effects

Accounting equation

Dual effect

Separate entity

- the owner of the business is a separate entity from the business.

Therefore:

- each transaction has both a debit and a credit entry in the ledger accounts.

- the amount invested into the business by the owner is kept separate, it is known as "capital". The amount withdrawn from the business by the owner for their own personal use, it is known as "drawings".
- Note: capital and drawings are not necessarily just cash, an owner can invest and withdraw other assets.

Accounting equation

Assets – Liabilities = Capital

Terminology

Asset
- something owned by the business

Liability
- something owed by the business

Capital
- amount the owner has invested in the business

Receivable
- someone who owes the business money

Payable
- someone the business owes money to

The accounting equation

Example

Accounting equation

(i) Ted pays £10,000 into a business bank account to start a business.

Dual effect	Assets (cash)	Capital
	£10,000	= £10,000

(ii) Ted buys goods to resell for £3,000 in cash

Dual effect	Assets + assets (cash) (inventory)	Capital
	£7,000 + £3,000	= £10,000

(iii) Ted sells the goods for cash for £4,000.

These goods were bought for £3,000, which is £1,000 less than what they have now been sold for. Therefore, a profit of £1,000 has been made.

This is added to the capital balance as it is an increase in the amount owed back to the owner of the business.

Dual effect	Assets (cash)	Capital	Profit
	£11,000	= £10,000	+ £1,000

(iv) Ted purchases more goods for £6,000 on credit

Dual effect	Assets (inventory)	Liabilities (payable)	Capital + Profit
	£11,000 + £6,000	− £6,000	= £11,000

(v) Ted sells these goods for £8,000 on credit

Dual effect	Assets (receivables)	− Liabilities	Capital + Profit
	£11,000 + £8,000	− £6,000 = £11,000	+ £2,000

(vi) Ted pays £500 of rent for his premises. This reduces his cash and profit by £500

Dual effect	Assets (cash)		Capital + Profit
	£10,500 + £8,000	− £6,000 = £11,000	+ £1,500

Types of income and expense

Capital income

Income received from the sale of non-current assets

Example: The proceeds received from selling a motor vehicle

Revenue income

Income received from the trading activities

Example: The proceeds received from selling goods (inventory)

Capital expenditure

Expense of acquiring or improving non-current assets

Examples: Buying a piece of machinery, removing single glazed windows and replacing with double glazed windows

Revenue expenditure

Day to day running expenses of the business, including the repair and maintenance of non-current assets.

Examples: Gas, electricity, rent, repairs and maintenance

3

Ledger accounting

- Ledger accounts.
- General rules of double entry bookkeeping.
- Accounting for cash transactions.
- Accounting for credit transactions.
- Balancing the ledger accounts.
- What is a trial balance?

Ledger accounts

Typical ledger account:

Title of account

Date	Narrative	£	Date	Narrative	£
	DEBIT side			CREDIT side	

The dual effect means that every transaction has a debit entry in one account and a credit entry in another account.

Key question – which account is the debit entry in and which account is the credit entry in?

Definition

A **cash transaction** means a transaction which is paid for immediately.

Definition

A **credit transaction** is a transaction that is only paid after an agreed period of time, e.g. 30 days.

Note that the terms 'cash' and 'cheque' are used interchangeably in the early part of your studies. If the person pays by cash or cheque, the money will be entered into the 'bank' account (sometimes called the 'cash account').

Thus if John buys a car for £4,000 and pays immediately with a cheque or cash, that is a cash transaction.

If John buys a car for £4,000 on credit, when he eventually pays he can pay with either cash or a cheque – it makes no difference – it will be a credit transaction.

General rules of double entry bookkeeping

The table below summarises the effect a debit (DR) or a credit (CR) entry can have.

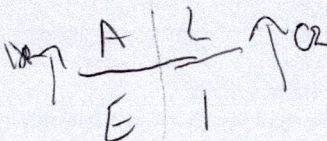

Ledger account	
DEBIT £	**CREDIT** £
Money in	Money out
Increase in asset	Increase in liability
Decrease in liability	Decrease in asset
Increase in expense	Increase in income

The mnemonic **DEAD CLIC** is a great way to remember the side to post a debit or credit entry to.

DRs increase;	CRs increase;
Expenses	Liabilities
Assets	Income
Drawings	Capital

Accounting for cash transactions

e.g **Example**

Cash transactions

(i) Payment of £10,000 into business bank account by owner:

Debit   Bank (money in)

Credit Capital (increase in liability – amount owed to owner)

Bank account		
	£	£
Capital	10,000	

Capital account		
	£	£
	Bank	10,000

(ii) Purchase of goods for cash of £3,000

Debit   Purchases (expense)

Credit Bank (money out)

Purchases account		
	£	£
Bank	3,000	

Bank account		
	£	£
	Purchases	3,000

(iii) Sale of goods for cash of £4,000
  Debit Bank (money in)
  Credit Sales (income)

Bank account				Sales account			
	£		£		£		£
Sales	4,000					Bank	4,000

(iv) Payment of rent in cash £500
  Debit   Rent (expense)
  Credit Bank (money out)

Rent account				Bank account			
	£		£		£		£
Bank	500					Rent	500

Accounting for credit transactions

(i) Purchases goods for £6,000 on credit
    Debit   Purchases (expense)
    Credit Payables (liability)

Purchases account			
	£		£
Payables	6,000		

Payables account			
	£		£
		Purchases	6,000

(ii) Sale of goods on credit for £8,000
    Debit   Receivables (asset)
    Credit Sales (income)

Receivables account			
	£		£
Sales	8,000		

Sales account			
	£		£
		Receivables	8,000

KAPLAN PUBLIS

(iii) Payment of part of money owed to credit supplier of £1,500

Debit   Payables (reduction in liability)
Credit Bank (money out)

Payables account				
	£			£
Bank	1,500			

Bank account				
	£			£
			Payables	1,500

(iv) Receipt of part of money owed by credit customer of £5,000

Debit   Bank (money in)
Credit Receivables (reduction in asset)

Bank account				
	£			£
Receivables	5,000			

Receivables account				
	£			£
			Bank	5,000

Balancing the ledger accounts

At various points in time the owner/owners of a business will need information about the total transactions in the period. E.g. total sales, amount of payables outstanding, amount of cash remaining. This can be found by balancing the ledger accounts.

e.g

Example

Here is a typical cash (or bank) account:

Cash account

	£		£
Capital	10,000	Purchases	3,000
Sales	4,000	Rent	500
Receivables	5,000	Payables	1,500

Step 1	Total both the debit side and the credit side and make a note of the totals.
Step 2	The higher of the totals should be inserted at the bottom of

both the debit side and the credit side (leaving a line before inserting the totals).

Cash account

	£		£
Capital	10,000	Purchases	3,000
Sales	4,000	Rent	500
Receivables	5,000	Payables	1,500
	19,000		19,000

Step 3	On the side that amounts to the lower total, insert the figure that makes that side add up to the higher total. This balance should have the narrative "balance carried down" ("balance c/d").

KAPLAN PUBLIS

Cash account

	£		£
Capital	10,000	Purchases	3,000
Sales	4,000	Rent	500
Receivables	5,000	Payables	1,500
		Balance c/d	14,000
	19,000		19,000

Step 4 On the opposite side to where the "balance carried down" has been inserted, enter the same figure below the total line. This should be referred to as "balance brought down" ("balance b/d").

Cash account

	£		£
Capital	10,000	Purchases	3,000
Sales	4,000	Rent	500
Receivables	5,000	Payables	1,500
		Balance c/d	14,000
	19,000		19,000
Balance b/d	14,000		

This shows that after all of these transactions there is £14,000 of cash left as an asset in the business (a debit balance brought down = an asset).

What is a trial balance?

- list of all of the ledger balances in the general ledger
- debit balances and credit balances listed separately
- debit balance total should equal credit balance total.

e.g

Example

Trial balance

	Debit balances £	Credit balances £
Sales		5,000
Wages	100	
Purchases	3,000	
Rent	200	
Car	3,000	
Receivables	100	
Payables		1,400
	_____	_____
	6,400	6,400
	_____	_____

Debit or credit balance?

If you are just given a list of balances you must know whether they are debit or credit balances.

Remember the rules!

Debit balances	Credit balances
Asset	Liability
Expense	Income
Drawings	Capital

4

Accounting for credit sales, VAT and discounts

- Accounting for credit sales.
- VAT and discounts.
- Accounting for credit sales returns.

Accounting for credit sales

The double entry for a sale including VAT:

Dr	Receivables	X	(gross – VAT inclusive)
Cr	VAT (sales tax)	X	(VAT)
Cr	Sales	X	(net – VAT exclusive)

VAT and discounts

A trade discount or a bulk discount is a definite reduction to the list price of a product or service. These discounts will be deducted prior to VAT being calculated.

A prompt payment discount is merely offered to the customer on the invoice. No deduction to the invoice value or to the VAT calculation takes place until the customer takes advantage of this discount by making payment within the required time.

e.g

Example

Goods are despatched to a customer with a list price of £1,000. The customer is allowed a trade discount of 20% and is offered a prompt payment discount of 4% if the invoice is paid within 10 days.

Invoice amounts:

	£
List price	1,000.00
Less: trade discount	(200.00)
	800.00
VAT (see below)	160.00
Invoice total	960.00
VAT calculation	£800 x 20%

NB The VAT has been calculated based on £800 (list price less trade discount).

Accounting for credit sales returns

The double entry for a sales return including VAT (sales tax) is:

Dr	Sales returns	X (net – VAT exclusive)
Dr	VAT (sales tax)	X (VAT)
Cr	Receivables	X (gross – VAT inclusive)

5

Accounting for credit purchases, VAT and discounts

- Accounting for credit purchases.
- VAT and discounts.
- Accounting for credit purchases returns.

Accounting for credit purchases

The double entry for a purchase including VAT:

Dr	Purchases	X	(net – VAT exclusive)
Dr	VAT (sales tax)	X	(VAT)
Cr	Payables	X	(gross – VAT inclusive)

VAT and discounts

VAT and discounts have already been studied when considering sales in chapter 4. The calculations of VAT and discounts are exactly the same when considering purchases.

The purchaser receives a "sales invoice" from the seller but the purchaser refers to this as a "purchase invoice" and enters it into the books accordingly. It is the same document but is referred to differently by the different parties involved in the transaction.

Ensure that you are happy with the calculations of VAT and discounts by reviewing over these in chapter 4.

Accounting for credit purchases returns

The double entry for a purchases return including VAT (sales tax) is:

Dr	Payables	X	(gross – VAT inclusive)
Cr	VAT (sales tax)	X	(VAT)
Cr	Purchases returns	X	(net – VAT exclusive)

Control accounts and subsidiary ledgers

- Introduction.
- Sales ledger control account.
- Posting the sales day book.
- Posting the sales returns day book.
- Purchases ledger control account.
- Posting the purchases day book.
- Posting the purchases returns day book.

Introduction

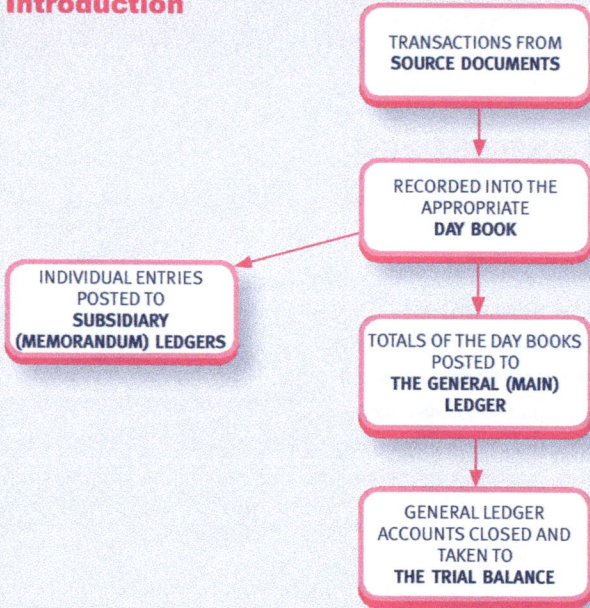

Sales ledger control account

- total receivables account
- sales invoices posted from sales day book
- credit notes posted from sales returns day book
- receipts from customers posted from cash receipts book
- discounts allowed to customers posted from discounts allowed day book (or from the cash receipts book if no discounts allowed day book maintained).

Posting the sales day book

General ledger

- at the end of each day/week/month SDB is totalled
- totals must then be posted to accounts in the general ledger.

Double entry:

Debit	Sales ledger Control account	Total (gross) figure
Credit	Sales account	Net figure
Credit	VAT account	VAT amount

SALES DAY BOOK

Date	Invoice No	Customer Name	Sales ledger code	Total (gross) £	VAT £	Net £
12/08/X3	69489	TJ Builder	SL21	2,004.12	334.02	1,670.10
12/08/X3	69490	McCarthy & Sons	SL08	1,485.74	247.62	1,238.12
12/08/X3	69491	Trevor Partner	SL10	1,063.10	177.18	885.92
				4,552.96	758.82	3,794.14

Debit sales ledger control account

Credit VAT

Credit sales

Sales Ledger Control Account

	£		£
SDB	4,552.96		

Sales account

	£		£
		SDB	3,794.14

VAT

	£		£
		SDB	758.82

Subsidiary (sales) ledger

- SLCA records the amount owing by all of the business's credit customers in total
- but also need information about each individual credit customer's balance
- therefore ledger account kept for each individual customer in a subsidiary ledger, the subsidiary (sales) ledger.

Subsidiary (sales) ledger

Customer A

£		£

Customer B

£		£

Customer C

£		£

Posting to the subsidiary (sales) ledger

- each individual entry from the sales day book must be entered into the relevant customer account in the subsidiary (sales) ledger
- amount entered is the gross invoice total (including VAT)
- entered on the debit side of the account indicating that this is the amount the receivable owes.

Example

Now we return to the sales day book from earlier and post the individual entries to the subsidiary (sales) ledger.

TJ Builder

	£		£
SDB	2,004.12		

McCarthy & Sons

	£		£
SDB	1,485.74		

Trevor Partner

	£		£
SDB	1,063.10		

Posting the sales returns day book

General ledger

- as with the SDB the SRDB must also be posted to the general ledger accounts and subsidiary (sales) ledger accounts.

Double entry:

Debit   Sales returns account   Net figure
Debit   VAT account   VAT total
Credit Sales Ledger
         Control Account   Total (gross) figure

SALES RETURNS DAY BOOK

Date	Credit Note No.	Customer Name	Code	Total (gross) £	VAT £	Net £
28/08/X3	03561	Trevor Partner	SL10	125.48	20.91	104.57
28/08/X3	03562	TJ Builder	SL21	151.74	25.29	126.45
				277.22	46.20	231.02

Credit sales ledger control account

Debit VAT

Debit sales returns

Sales ledger control account

	£		£
SDB	4,552.96	SRDB	277.22

Sales account

	£		£
		SDB	3,794.14

VAT account

	£		£
SRDB	46.20	SDB	758.82

Sales returns account

	£		£
SRDB	231.02		

Subsidiary (sales) ledger

Each individual credit note must be entered in the customer's account:

- gross credit note total
- credit individual receivable account (reducing the amount owed).

T J Builder

	£		£
SDB	2,004.12	SRDB	151.74

McCarthy & Sons

	£		£
SDB	1,485.74		

Trevor Partner

	£		£
SDB	1,063.10	SRDB	125.48

Purchases ledger control account

- total payables account
- purchase invoices posted from purchases day book
- credit notes posted from purchases returns day book
- payments to suppliers posted from cash payments book
- discounts received from suppliers posted from discounts received day book (or from cash payments book if no discount received day book maintained).

Posting the purchases day book (PDB)

General ledger

- at the end of each day/week/month PDB is totalled
- totals must then be posted to accounts in the general ledger.

Double entry:

Debit	Purchases account	Net figure
Debit	VAT account amount	VAT
Credit	Purchases ledger Control account (PLCA)	Total (gross) figure

PURCHASES DAY BOOK

Date	Invoice No.	Code	Supplier	Total (gross) £	VAT £	Net £
20X1						
7 May	2814	PL06	J Taylor	190.41	31.73	158.68
8 May	2815	PL13	McMinn Partners	288.14	48.02	240.12
	2816	PL27	D B Bros	96.54	16.09	80.45
9 May	2817	PL03	J S Ltd	221.58	36.93	184.65
				796.67	132.77	663.90

Credit purchases ledger control account

Debit VAT

Debit purchases

Purchases account

	£		£
PDB	663.90		

VAT account

	£		£
PDB	132.77		

Purchases ledger control account

	£		£
		PDB	796.67

Subsidiary purchases ledger

- the PLCA records the amount owing to all of the business's credit suppliers in total
- but also need information about each individual credit supplier's balance
- therefore ledger account kept for each individual supplier in a subsidiary ledger, the subsidiary (purchases) ledger.

Subsidiary (Purchases) Ledger

Supplier A

	£		£

Supplier B

	£		£

Supplier C

	£		£

Posting to the subsidiary (purchases) ledger

- each individual entry from the purchases day book must be entered into the relevant supplier account in the subsidiary (purchases) ledger
- amount entered is the gross invoice total (including VAT)
- entered on the credit side of the account indicating that this is the amount owed to the supplier.

Example continued

Now we return to the purchases day book from earlier and post the individual entries to the subsidiary (purchases) ledger.

J Taylor			
£			£
		PDB	190.41

D B Bros			
£			£
		PDB	96.54

McMinn Partners			
£			£
		PDB	288.14

J S Ltd			
£			£
		PDB	221.58

Posting the purchases returns day book (PRDB)

PURCHASES RETURNS DAY BOOK						
Date	Credit note no	Supplier	Code	Total (gross) £	VAT £	Net £
09/05/X1	02456	McMinn Partners	PL13	64.80	10.80	54.00
09/05/X1	02457	J S Ltd	PL03	72.00	12.00	60.00
				136.80	22.80	114.00

Debit purchases ledger control account

Credit VAT

Credit purchases returns

General ledger

- as with the PDB the PRDB must also be posted to the general ledger accounts and subsidiary (purchases) ledger accounts.

Double entry:

Debit	Purchases ledger Control account	Total (gross) figure
Credit	Purchases returns account	Net figure
Credit	VAT account total	VAT

Purchases account

	£		£
PDB	663.90		

VAT account

	£		£
PDB	132.77	PRDB	22.80

Purchase Ledger Control Account

	£		£
PRDB	136.80	PDB	796.67

Purchases returns account

	£		£
		PRDB	114.00

Subsidiary (purchases) ledger

Each individual credit note must be entered in the supplier's account:

- gross credit note total

debit individual supplier account (reducing the amount owing).

J Taylor

	£		£
		PDB	190.41

McMinn Partners

	£		£
PRDB	64.80	PDB	288.14

D B Bros

	£		£
		PDB	96.54

J S Ltd

	£		£
PRDB	72.00	PDB	221.58

Receipts and payments

- Receivables statements.
- Aged debt analysis.
- Posting the cash receipts book and the discounts allowed book to the general ledger.
- Posting the discounts allowed day book.
- Posting the cash receipts book and discounts allowed book to the subsidiary ledger.
- Checks to make on purchase invoices.
- Posting the cash payments book and discounts received book to the general ledger.
- Posting the discounts received day book.
- Posting the cash payments book and discounts received book to the subsidiary ledger.
- The cash book as part of the general ledger.
- Petty cash
  - system
  - vouchers
  - book.
- Posting the petty cashbook.
- Reconciling petty cash.
- Petty cash control account
  - reconciliation.

Receivables' statements

- sent by supplier to customer usually monthly
- reminder of amounts due.

INVOICE				
Invoice to Fitch & Partners 23 Emma Place Manchester M6 4TZ		NICK BROOKS 225 School Lane Weymouth, Dorset WE36 5NR Tel: 0149 29381 Fax: 0149 29382 Date: 30/04/X2		
Date	Transaction	Debit £	Credit £	Balance £
03/04	INV001	185.65		185.65
10/04	CN001		49.35	136.30
14/04	INV005	206.80		343.10
18/04	PAYMENT		136.30	206.80
21/04	INV007	253.80		460.60
26/04	INV008	192.70		653.30

May we remind you that our credit terms are 30 days
With 3% discount for payment within 14 days

Aged debt analysis

- internal document
- prepared for each individual customer
- shows the age of amounts outstanding
- useful for identifying slow paying/problem customers.

Customer	Total £	<30 days £	30 to 60 days £	>60 days £
H Hardy	689.46	368.46	321.00	–
L Framer	442.79	379.60	–	63.19
K Knight	317.68	–	169.46	148.22

Posting the cash receipts book and the discounts allowed book to the general ledger

Basic double entry for cash receipts:

Debit	Bank account
Credit	Sales Ledger Control Account
	(receipts from receivables)
	Sales (cash sales)
	Other income (e.g. rent)

In most cases the cash receipts book is not only a book of prime entry but also part of the general ledger in which case the debit entry for the total column is not required.

Double entry for discount allowed:

Debit	Discount allowed
Debit	VAT
Credit	Sales Ledger Control Account

Postings

Cash receipts book						
Date	Narrative	Total £	VAT £	Receivables £	Cash sales £	Sundry £
3 Jul	A Brown	20.54	3.42		17.12	
5 Jul	S Smith & Co Ltd	9.30		9.30		
	P Priest	60.80		60.80		
	James & Jeans	39.02	6.50		32.52	
	LS Moore	17.00		17.00		
6 Jul	L White Ltd	5.16		5.16		
7 Jul	M N Furnishers Ltd	112.58				112.58
	R B Roberts	23.65		23.65		
	Light and Shade	86.95		86.95		
		375.00	9.92	202.86	49.64	112.58

Credit VAT account

Credit sales ledger control account

Credit sales account

Credit sundry income account

Posting the discounts allowed day book

Discounts allowed book					
Date	Narrative	Reference	Total £	VAT £	Net £
Totals					

Cr Sales ledger control account

Dr VAT

Dr Discount allowed

Posting the cash receipts book and discounts allowed book to the subsidiary ledger

- after the totals have been posted to the general ledger from the cash receipts book the individual entries in the receivables column must be posted to the subsidiary (sales) ledger
- each cash receipt is credited to the individual receivable account (reduction of amount owing)
- each discount allowed is credited to the individual receivable account (reduction of amount owing).

Subsidiary sales ledger – postings (extracts

Smith & Co Ltd

£		
	CRB	9.30

L S Moore

£		
	CRB	17.00
	DAB	1.00

The cash receipts from Smith & Co and L S Moore have been taken from the cash receipts book. L S Moore received a prompt payment discount of £1.00 (gross).

Checks to make on purchase invoices

Once a purchase invoice is received from a supplier a number of checks must be made on it to ensure that it is valid before it is authorised for payment.

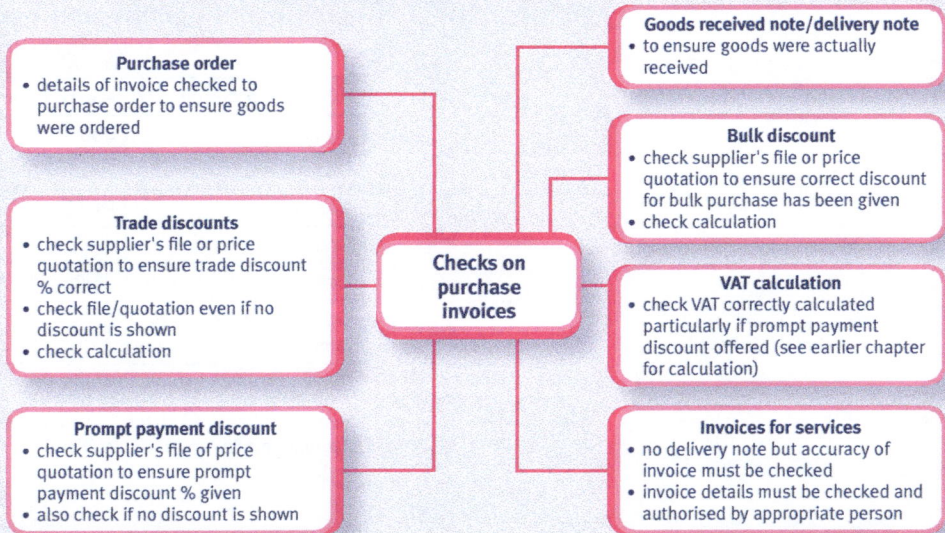

Purchase order
- details of invoice checked to purchase order to ensure goods were ordered

Goods received note/delivery note
- to ensure goods were actually received

Trade discounts
- check supplier's file or price quotation to ensure trade discount % correct
- check file/quotation even if no discount is shown
- check calculation

Checks on purchase invoices

Bulk discount
- check supplier's file or price quotation to ensure correct discount for bulk purchase has been given
- check calculation

VAT calculation
- check VAT correctly calculated particularly if prompt payment discount offered (see earlier chapter for calculation)

Prompt payment discount
- check supplier's file of price quotation to ensure prompt payment discount % given
- also check if no discount is shown

Invoices for services
- no delivery note but accuracy of invoice must be checked
- invoice details must be checked and authorised by appropriate person

Credit notes

The same checks as above should be made on credit notes received from suppliers.

Example of authorisation stamp

Account code is purchase ledger code

Purchase order no	436129
Invoice No	388649
Cheque no	
Account code	PL70
Checked	J Wilmber
Date	03/05/X4
General ledger account	

Cheque number inserted when payment made

Signed when all checks are made on invoice

When the invoice has been authorised, the amount to be paid must be calculated. This may also include accounting for prompt payment discount as considered previously.

e.g

Example

An invoice is received from a supplier as follows:

	£
List price	1,000.00
Trade discount	(200.00)
	800.00
VAT	160.00
	960.00

A 4% prompt payment discount is offered for payment within 14 days.

If the prompt payment discount is taken - the amount paid will be £960 less 4% which equals £921.60. This is made up of a revised net amount of £768 and a revised VAT charge of £153.60.

Payment by invoice
- each invoice paid at latest date allowed by credit terms
- must ensure that if the business policy is to take cash discounts then invoice is paid in time to reach supplier within agreed period

Payment on set date
- this may be one day per week/month but this may mean that cash discounts are lost
- alternative to set day per week/fortnight when all invoices which will have exceeded credit/settlement discount limit by following payment date are paid

Methods of scheduling of payments

Payment of supplier's statements
- received monthly showing invoices outstanding
- must be checked to supplier's account to ensure correct
- invoices on statement will be paid according to business policy
- often remittance advice attached to statement to show amounts being paid

Posting the cash payments book and the discounts received book to the general ledger

Basic double entry for cash payments :

Debit	Purchases for cash
Debit	Purchases ledger control account
Debit	Other expenses
Credit	Bank account

In most cases the cash payments book is not only a book of prime entry but also part of the general ledger in which case the credit entry for the total column is not required.

Double entry for discount received:

Debit	Purchases ledger control account
Credit	Discount received
Credit	VAT

Postings

Date	Details	Cheque No	Total	VAT £	Purchase ledger £	Cash purchases £	Post £
14/2	K Ellis	1152	80.00		80.00		
15/2	Hutt Ltd	1153	120.00	20.00		100.00	
16/2	Biggs Ltd	1154	200.00				200.00
			400.00	20.00	80.00	100.00	200.00

Cash payments book

Debit VAT account

Debit purchases ledger control account

Debit cash purchases

Debit post

Posting the discounts received day book

Discounts received book					
Date	Narrative	Reference	Total £	VAT £	Net £
Totals					

Dr Purchases ledger control account

Cr VAT

Cr Discount received

Posting the cash payments book and discounts received book to the subsidiary ledger

- after the totals have been posted to the general ledger from the cash payments book the individual entries in the purchase ledger column must be posted to the subsidiary (purchases) ledger
- each cash payment is debited to the individual payable account (reduction of amount owing)
- each discount received is debited to the individual payable account (reduction of amount owing).

Subsidiary (purchases) ledger – postings (extracts)

K Ellis		
	£	£
CPB	80.00	
DRB	2.00	

K Ellis payment of £80.00 was detailed in the cash payments book. A discount received of £2.00 (gross) was also recorded.

The cash book as part of the general ledger

The two sides of the cash book which are the cash receipts and the cash payments have been reviewed already as separate books.

The assessment often shows the cashbook as a ledger account format. This means that the cashbook actually forms a part of the general ledger, with the entries being one side of the double entry required within the general ledger.

The requirement will be to complete the other side of the entry within the general ledger, and to update the individual accounts in the subsidiary ledger.

Petty cash system

Most businesses require small amounts of cash for small cash expenses and reimbursement of business expenditure incurred by employees.

Petty cash box
- must be locked
- only petty cashier has access.

> Employee incurs expense e.g. purchase stamps for office

⬇

> Fills out petty cash voucher for amount and attaches receipt

⬇

> Takes to petty cashier who checks voucher and receipt and authorises voucher

⬇

> Petty cashier gives employee amount spent out of petty cash box and puts voucher in petty cash box

⬇

> Voucher is recorded in petty cash book

Imprest system

- most common system of controlling petty cash
- set amount of petty cash for period determined e.g. £100 per week
- cash paid out only when vouchers put into petty cash box
- at end of week petty cash box topped back up to £100 from bank account.

Monday	Friday	Friday
Petty cash box	Petty cash box	Petty cash box
£100 cash	£30 cash £70 vouchers	£100 (£70 withdrawn in cash from bank account. Vouchers removed and filed).

Non-imprest system

- another system of dealing with petty cash
- for example a set amount, say £100, being withdrawn in cash and put into the petty cash box each week no matter how much is paid out.

Problems

More than £100 spent – petty cash runs out

Less than £100 spent – petty cash builds up over time

Petty cash vouchers

- gives details of expenditure incurred by employee
- must normally be supported by receipt or other evidence of expense
- must include VAT for expense where VAT is reclaimable
- must be authorised before payment can be made.

Signature of employee claiming petty cash

Sequential petty cash voucher number

Signature of person authorising voucher

Date and details of expenditure

Total amount paid to employee

PETTY CASH VOUCHER		
Authorised by	**Received by**	**No.** 4173
F R Clarke	I Kent	
Date	**Description**	**Amount**
4 April	Train Fare	12 50
	Total	12 50

Petty cash book

- book of prime entry
- often part of general ledger as well
- small cash receipts side
- larger analysed cash payments side.

PETTY CASH BOOK											
Receipts			Payments								
Date	Narrative	Total £	Date	Narrative	Voucher no	Total £	Postage £	Cleaning £	Tea & Coffee £	Sundry £	VAT £
1 Nov	Bal b/f	35.50									
1 Nov	Cheque	114.50	1 Nov	ASDA	58	23.50			23.50		
			2 Nov	Post Office Ltd	59	29.50	29.50				
			2 Nov	Cleaning materials	60	15.07		12.56			2.51
			3 Nov	Postage	61	16.19	16.19				
			3 Nov	ASDA	62	10.57		8.81			1.76
			4 Nov	Newspapers	63	18.90				18.90	
			5 Nov	ASDA	64	12.10				10.09	2.01
						125.83	45.69	21.37	23.50	28.99	6.28

Receipts side – only one column as only entry is regular payment in cash from bank

Payments side – analysed according to typical expenditure plus VAT column

Imprest amount of £150 to start week

Date of claim

Details

Sequential petty cash voucher numbers

Analysed payments – total column includes VAT but analysis column amount is net of VAT

When petty cash book has been written up for a period it must be totalled. Totals should then be checked by cross-casting:

	£
Postage	45.69
Cleaning	21.37
Tea & coffee	23.50
Sundry	28.99
VAT	6.28
Total	125.83

Topping up the petty cash box

- at the end of the period (in this case a week) the petty cash box will be topped up to the imprest amount
- this is done by taking cash out of the bank account
- amount is total of the petty cash expenditure – £125.83
- petty cash box should then have imprest amount of £150 in order to start following week.

Posting the petty cash book (PCB)

e.g

Petty cash book part of general ledger

- petty cash book is normally part of the general ledger.

Receipt of cash

- debit entry already in petty cash book
- only posting required is a credit in the cash payments book for the cash taken out of the bank (this should have been done from cheque stub anyway).

Petty cash payments

- credit entry in petty cash book (total column £125.83)
- debit entries required for each expense account and VAT account.

Postage account		
	£	£
PCB	45.69	

Cleaning account		
	£	£
PCB	21.37	

Food and drink account		
	£	£
PCB	23.50	

Sundry expenses account		
	£	£
PCB	28.99	

VAT account		
	£	£
PCB	6.28	

Petty cash book not part of general ledger

- if the petty cash book is not part of the general ledger then a petty cash control account is required in the general ledger.

Petty cash receipt

- receipt of cash at start of week

    Debit Petty cash

           control account £114.50

    Credit Bank account   £114.50

Petty cash payments

    Debit Postage   £45.69

           Cleaning   £21.37

           Food and drink £23.50

           Sundry expenses £28.99

           VAT   £ 6.28

    Credit Petty cash

           control account   £125.83

Reconciling petty cash

Under imprest system:

Total of cash in petty cash box	+	Total of vouchers in petty cash box	=	Imprest amount

Therefore to check petty cash security:

- total cash in box
- total vouchers in box
- add together
- should equal imprest amount
- vouchers then removed from box, entered into petty cash book and filed.

Petty cash control account

If the petty cash book is not part of the general ledger there will be a petty cash control account in the general ledger which shows the summarised cash receipts and payments for the period.

Example

A petty cash system is run on an imprest system of £100. During the month of May petty cash expenditure totalled £68 and the petty cash box was topped back up to the imprest amount with a withdrawal of £68 cash from the bank.

Step 1 – Enter the imprest amount that would have been in the petty cash box at the start of the month – asset – debit balance.

Petty cash control account

	£		£
Opening balance	100		

Step 2 – Enter the total paid out in the month.

Petty cash control account

	£		£
Opening balance	100	Petty cash payments	68

Full double entry:

    Debit   Expense accounts

    Credit Petty cash control account

Step 3 – Enter the cash paid into petty cash from the bank.

Petty cash control account

	£		£
Opening balance	100	Petty cash payments	68
Cash	68		

Full double entry:

    Debit   Petty cash control account

    Credit Cash payments book

Step 4 – Carry down the balance at the end of the month – the imprest amount.

Petty cash control account

	£		£
Opening balance	100	Petty cash payments	68
Cash	68	Balance c/d	100
	168		168
Balance b/d	100		

Asset – debit balance

Topping up the petty cash box

- at the end of the period (in this case a week) the petty cash box will be topped up to the imprest amount
- this is done by taking cash out of the bank account
- amount is total of the petty cash expenditure – £68.00
- petty cash box should then have imprest amount of £100 in order to start following week.

Petty cash control account reconciliation

- at the end of a period the balance on the petty cash control account should equal the amount of cash in the petty cash box
- any difference must be investigated.

Differences

More cash than balance	Less cash than balance
• error in writing up petty cash book	• error in writing up cash book
• less cash given out than should have been	• too much cash given out than should have been
	• petty cash voucher omitted from petty cash book
	• cash paid out without voucher
	• cash could have been stolen

Errors and suspense accounts

- What is a trial balance?
- Errors.
- Journal entries.
- Suspense account.
- Correcting errors and clearing the suspense account.

What is a trial balance?

- list of all of the ledger balances in the general ledger
- debit balances and credit balances listed in separate columns
- the total of the debit balances should equal the total of the credit balances.

Example

Trial balance

	Debit balances £	Credit balances £
Sales		5,000
Wages	100	
Purchases	3,000	
Rent	200	
Car	3,000	
Receivables	100	
Payables		1,400
	6,400	6,400

Debit or credit balance?

If you are just given a list of balances you must know whether they are debit or credit balances.

Remember the rules!

Debit balances	Credit balances
Expense	Liability
Asset	Income
Drawings	Capital

Errors

In a manual accounting system errors will be made – some are identified by extracting a trial balance but others are not.

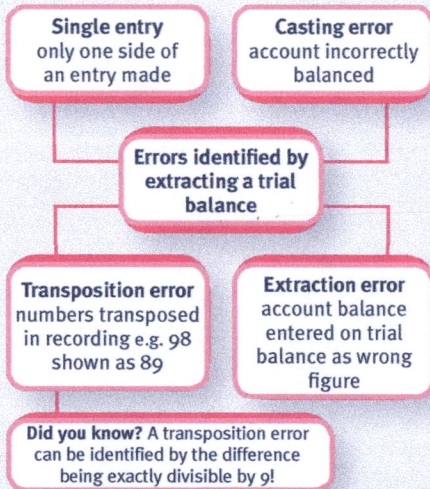

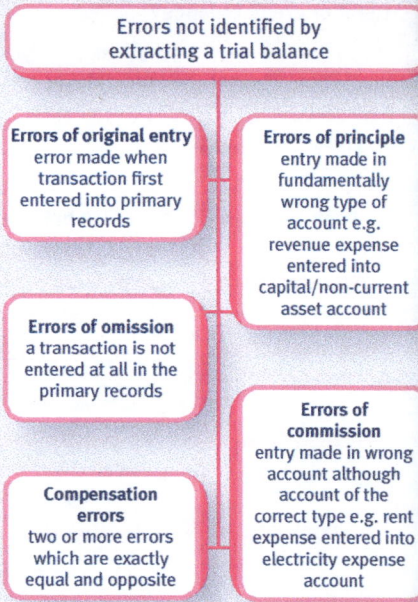

Errors not identified by extracting a trial balance

Errors of original entry
error made when transaction first entered into primary records

Errors of principle
entry made in fundamentally wrong type of account e.g. revenue expense entered into capital/non-current asset account

Errors of omission
a transaction is not entered at all in the primary records

Errors of commission
entry made in wrong account although account of the correct type e.g. rent expense entered into electricity expense account

Compensation errors
two or more errors which are exactly equal and opposite

Single entry
only one side of an entry made

Casting error
account incorrectly balanced

Errors identified by extracting a trial balance

Transposition error
numbers transposed in recording e.g. 98 shown as 89

Extraction error
account balance entered on trial balance as wrong figure

Did you know? A transposition error can be identified by the difference being exactly divisible by 9!

Journal entries

- written instruction to bookkeeper to put through a double entry which has not been sourced from the books of prime entry
- used for correction of errors/adjustments/ unusual items
- only used for adjusting double entry errors in the general ledger – not used for entries in the subsidiary sales or purchases ledgers.

Journal entry		No: 06671		
Prepared by	P Freer			
Authorised by	P Simms			
Date:	8 May 20X1			
Narrative: To write off irrecoverable debt from L. C. Hamper				
Account		Code	Debit £	Credit £
Irrecoverable debt expense		ML05	102.00	
SLCA		ML06		102.00
			102.00	102.00

Authorisation

Reason for journal

Double entry

Sequential journal number

Equal totals as journal must balance

Suspense account

Used in two circumstances

Bookkeeper does not know one side of an entry therefore posts it to a suspense account

When trial balance totals disagree used to temporarily balance the trial balance

Example
£200 received but bookkeeper does not know what it is for so debits cash receipts book and credits suspense account

Example
Total of debit balances on trial balance is £35,000 but total of credit balances is £34,000. 1,000 credited to suspense account to make trial balance totals equal

Correcting errors and clearing the suspense account

* errors corrected by putting through a journal for the correcting entry.

How to find correcting entry

* work out the double entry that has been done
* work out the double entry that should have been done
* draft journal entry to go from what has been done to what should have been done.

Example

journal entries

(i) An amount of £200 for electricity bill payments was entered into the rent account.

What has been done?

Debit	Rent account	£200
Credit	Bank account	£200

What should have been done?

Debit	Electricity account	£200
Credit	Bank account	£200

How do we correct it? – Journal entry

Debit	Electricity account	£200
Credit	Rent account	£200

(ii) A purchase invoice for £1,000 had not been entered into the books of prime entry.

What has been done?

No entries at all

What should have been done?

Debit	Purchases account	£1,000
Credit	Purchases ledger control account	£1,000

How do we correct it? – Journal entry

Debit	Purchases account	£1,000
Credit	Purchases ledger control account	£1,000

(iii) An irrecoverable debt for £100 is to
be written off.

This is not correction of an error but an
adjustment to be made.

Journal entry

| Debit | Irrecoverable debt expense account | £100 |
| Credit | Sales ledger control account | £100 |

(iv) A contra entry for £500 has been
entered in the general ledger control
accounts but has not been entered in
the subsidiary (purchases) ledger.

No journal entry is required as the error
is not in the general ledger but the
subsidiary ledger. However the payable's
account in the subsidiary (purchases)
ledger must be debited to reflect this
contra entry.

Errors and the suspense account

Some errors made will affect the trial balance
and therefore are part of the suspense
account balance.

Example

(i) Discounts allowed of £150 have been entered as a credit entry in the discounts allowed account

What has been done?

| Credit | Discount allowed account | £150 |
| Credit | Sales ledger control account | £150 |

What should have been done?

| Debit | Discount allowed account | £150 |
| Credit | Sales ledger control account | £150 |

How do we correct it? – Journal entry

| Debit | Discount allowed account | £300 |
| Credit | Suspense account | £300 |

The discount allowed account has been credited rather than debited with £150 therefore to turn this into a debit of £150 it needs to be debited with £300. No other account is incorrect so the other side of the entry is to the suspense account.

(ii) The balance for motor expenses of £400 has been omitted from the trial balance.

What has been done?

The motor expenses balance of £400 has been omitted from the trial balance.

What should be done?

A £400 debit balance (expense) must appear on the trial balance.

How do we correct it? – Journal entry

Debit Motor expenses (TB) £400
Credit Suspense account £400

Clearing the suspense account

The suspense account cannot remain as a permanent account and must eventually be investigated and cleared.

Example

A business has a suspense account with a debit balance of £80.

The following errors were noted:

(i) rent of £750 was entered into the rent account as £570

(ii) an advertising bill of was overstated in the advertising account by £100

Journals

(i) Debit   Rent account   £180

     Credit Suspense account £180

(ii) Debit   Suspense account £100

     Credit Advertising account £100

Suspense account

	£		£
Opening balance	80		
Advertising	100	Rent	180
	180		180

The suspense account is now cleared.

9

Control account reconciliations

- Sales ledger control account.
- Sales ledger control account reconciliation.
- Purchases ledger control account.
- Purchases ledger control account reconciliation.
- VAT control accounts.

Sales ledger control account

- total receivables account
- sales invoices posted from sales day book
- credit notes posted from sales returns day book
- receipts from customers posted from cash receipts book.

Example

Writing up the sales ledger control account

The opening balance at 1 May on the sales ledger control account is £3,400.

Sales ledger control account

	£		£
Opening balance	3,400		

Asset – debit balance

- total from sales day book for month of May £20,600

Sales ledger control account

	£		£
Opening balance	3,400		
SDB	20,600		

Full double entry:

Debit   Sales ledger control account

Credit Sales and VAT accounts

- total from sales returns day book for month of May £1,800

Sales ledger control account

	£		£
Opening balance	3,400	SRDB	1,800
SDB	20,600		

Full double entry:

Debit   **Sales returns and VAT accounts**

Credit   **Sales ledger control account**

- total from receivables column in cash receipts book of £19,500

Sales ledger control account

	£		£
Opening balance	3,400	SRDB	1,800
SDB	20,600	CRB	19,500

Full double entry:

Debit   **Cash book**

Credit   **Sales ledger control account**

- total of discounts allowed column in Discount allowed Daybook (DADB) £1,200.

Sales ledger control account

	£		£
Opening balance	3,400	SRDB	1,800
SDB	20,600	CRB	19,500
		DADB	1,200

Full double entry:

Debit   **Discounts allowed account**

Credit **Sales ledger control account**

Other entries to the sales ledger control account

There are two other potential entries in the sales ledger control account:

- irrecoverable debts written off – when a debt is highly unlikely to be received
- contra entry – when money is owed to a supplier who is also a customer and therefore owes money – the two amounts are set off against each other.

Example

Irrecoverable debts written off

- a customer owing £400 has gone into liquidation and therefore it has been decided to write this debt off as bad.

Sales ledger control account

	£		£
Opening balance	3,400	SRDB	1,800
SDB	20,600	CRB	19,500
		DADB	1,200
		Irrecoverable debt expense	400

Full double entry:

Debit	Irrecoverable debt expense account
Credit	Sales ledger control account

Example continued – contra entry

- a customer who owes us £200 is also a supplier and we owe him £300. It has been agreed that the two amounts should be set off by a contra entry leaving only £100 owed by us to the supplier.

Sales ledger control account

	£		£
Opening balance	3,400	SRDB	1,800
SDB	20,600	CRB	19,500
		DADB	1,200
		Irrecoverable debt write off	400
		Contra	200

Full double entry:

Debit	Purchases ledger control account
Credit	Sales ledger control account

Example continued – balancing the sales ledger control account

Sales ledger control account

	£		£
Opening balance	3,400	SRDB	1,800
SDB	20,600	CRB	19,500
		DADB	1,200
		Irrecoverable debt write off	400
		Contra	200
		Balance c/d	900
	24,000		24,000
Balance b/d	900		

This shows that at the end of May we have total receivables of £900.

Sales ledger control account reconciliation

- the sales ledger control account is written up using totals from the sales day book, sales returns day book and cash receipts book

- individual accounts for receivables in the subsidiary (sales) ledger are written up using the individual entries from the sales day book, sales returns day book and cash receipts book

- as both are written up from the same sources of information, at the end of the period the balance on the sales ledger control account should equal the total of the list of balances in the subsidiary (sales) ledger.

| SLCA balance | = | Total of list of subsidiary (sales) ledger |

Purpose of sales ledger control account reconciliation

- to show that SLCA does in fact equal the total of the list of balances

- to indicate that there are errors in either the SLCA or the subsidiary (sales) ledger accounts if the two are not equal

- to find the correct figure for total receivables to appear in the trial balance.

Preparing a sales ledger control account reconciliation

Step 1

- Extract list of balances from subsidiary (sales) ledger accounts and total.

Step 2

- Balance the sales ledger control account.

Step 3

- If the two figures are different the reasons for the difference must be investigated.

Step 4

- correct any errors that affect the sales ledger control account
- find corrected balance on sales ledger control account.

Step 5

- correct any errors that affect the total of the list of balances from the subsidiary (sales) ledger
- find corrected total of list of subsidiary (sales) ledger balances.

e.g Example

Sales ledger control account reconciliation

The balance on the sales ledger control account at 31 May is £4,100. The individual balances on the subsidiary (sales) ledger are as follows:

	£
Receivable A	1,200
Receivable B	300
Receivable C	2,000
Receivable D	1,000

Step 1

- **Extract list of balances from subsidiary (sales) ledger accounts and total**

	£
Receivable A	1,200
Receivable B	300
Receivable C	2,000
Receivable D	1,000
	4,500

Step 2

- **Balance the sales ledger control account**

The balance has been given as £4,100.

Step 3

- **If the two figures are different the reasons for the difference must be investigated**

You are given the following information:

- a page of the sales day book had been undercast by £100

- a credit note for £50 to Receivable A had been entered into A's subsidiary (sales) ledger account as an invoice

- a contra entry with Receivable B for £200 had only been entered in the sales ledger control account and not the individual subsidiary (sales) ledger account.

Step 4

- correct any errors that affect the sales ledger control account

- find corrected balance on sales ledger control account.

Sales ledger control account

	£		£
Original balance	4,100		
SDB undercast	100	Correct balance	4,200
CPB	4,200		4,200
Correct balance	4,200		

If the sales day book was undercast then the amount posted to the sales ledger control account was £100 too small and therefore an additional debit entry for £100 is needed in the control account.

The other two adjustments affect the individual accounts not the control account.

Step 5

- correct any errors that affect the total of the list of balances from the subsidiary (sales) ledger

- find corrected total of list of subsidiary (sales) ledger balances.

	£
Total list of balances	4,500
Less: Credit note entered as invoice	(100)
Less: Contra	(200)
Corrected list of balances	4,200

As the credit note for £50 had been entered as an invoice, the list of balances must be reduced by £100 to reflect the removal of the invoice and the entry of the credit note.

The contra had only been entered in the sales ledger control account therefore £200 must be deducted from the list of balances.

Credit balances on sales ledger accounts

- normally a receivable's balance on his subsidiary (sales) ledger account will be a debit balance brought down

- sometimes however balance will be a credit balance.

Reasons for credit balance:

Overpayment by receivable

Misposting to subsidiary (sales) ledger account

Treatment of credit balance

- when the list of subsidiary (sales) ledger balances is drawn up and totalled, the credit balance must be deducted rather than added.

Purchases ledger control account

- total payables account
- purchase invoices posted from purchases day book
- credit notes posted from purchases returns day book
- payments to suppliers posted from cash payments book
- discounts received from discount received day book.

e.g

Example

Writing up the purchases ledger control account

- the opening balance at 1 May on the purchases ledger control account is £2,100

Purchases ledger control account

	£		£
		Opening balance	2,100

Liability – credit balance

- total from purchases day book for month of May £15,800

Purchases ledger control account

	£		£
		Opening balance	2,100
		PDB	15,800

Full double entry:

Debit Purchases and VAT accounts

Credit Purchases ledger control account

- total from purchases returns day book for month of May £900

Purchases ledger control account

	£		£
PRDB	900	Opening balance	2,100
		PDB	15,800

Full double entry:

Debit Purchases ledger control account

Credit Purchases returns and VAT accounts

- total from payables column in cash payments book of £13,000

Purchases ledger control account

	£		£
PRDB	900	Opening balance	2,100
CPB	13,000	PDB	15,800

Full double entry:

Debit **Purchases ledger control account**

Credit **Cash Book**

- total of discount received column in discount received daybook £700

Purchases ledger control account

	£		£
PRDB	900	Opening balance	2,100
CPB	13,000	PDB	15,800
DRDB	700		

Full double entry:

Debit **Purchases ledger control account**

Credit **Discount received account**

- a customer who owes us £200 is also a supplier and we owe him £300. It has been agreed that the two amounts should be set off by a contra entry leaving only £100 owed by us to the supplier.

Purchases ledger control account

	£		£
PRDB	900	Opening balance	2,100
CPB	13,000	PDB	15,800
DRDB	700		
Contra	200		

Full double entry:

Debit   **Purchases ledger control account**

Credit   **Sales ledger control account**

Balancing the purchases ledger control account

Purchases ledger control account

	£		£
PRDB	900	Opening balance	2,100
CPB	13,000	PDB	15,800
DRDB	700		
Contra	200		
Balance c/d	3,100		
	17,900		17,900
		Balance b/d	3,100

This shows that we have payables totalling £3,100 at the end of May.

Purchases ledger control account reconciliation

- the purchases ledger control account is written up using totals from the purchases day book, purchases returns day book and cash payments book

- individual accounts for payables in the subsidiary (purchases) ledger are written up using the individual entries from the purchases day book, purchases returns day book and cash payments book

- as both are written up from the same sources of information then at the end of the period the balance on the purchases ledger control account should equal the total of the list of balances in the subsidiary (purchases) ledger.

PLCA balance **=** Total of list of subsidiary (purchases) ledger

Purpose of purchases ledger control account reconciliation

- to show that the PLCA does in fact equal the total of the list of balances

- to indicate that there are errors in either the PLCA or the subsidiary (purchases) ledger accounts if the two are not equal

- to find the correct figure for total payables to appear in the trial balance.

Preparing a purchases ledger control account reconciliation

Step 1

- Extract list of balances from subsidiary (purchases) ledger accounts and total.

Step 2

- Balance the purchases ledger control account.

Step 3

- If the two figures are different the reasons for the difference must be investigated.

Step 4

- correct any errors that affect the purchases ledger control account
- find corrected balance on the purchases ledger control account.

Step 5

- correct any errors that affect the total of the list of balances from the subsidiary (purchases) ledger
- find corrected total of list of subsidiary (purchases) ledger balances.

e.g

Example

Purchases ledger control account reconciliation

The balance on the purchases ledger control account at 31 May is £2,000. The individual balances on the subsidiary (purchases) ledger are as follows:

	£
Payable E	800
Payable F	600
Payable G	400
Payable H	700

Step 1

- **Extract list of balances from subsidiary (purchases) ledger accounts and total**

	£
Payable E	800
Payable F	600
Payable G	400
Payable H	700
	2,500

Step 2

- **Balance the purchases ledger control account**

  The balance has been given as £2,000.

Step 3

- **If the two figures are different the reasons for the difference must be investigated.**

You are given the following information:

- a page of the purchases returns day book had been overcast by £1,000

- discounts received from suppliers totalling £680 had not been posted to the control account

- an invoice to payable G for £350 had been entered into the individual account in the subsidiary (purchases) ledger as £530.

Step 4

- correct any errors that affect the purchases ledger control account
- find corrected balance on purchases ledger control account.

Purchases ledger control account

	£		£
Discounts received	680	Original balance	2,000
Corrected balance	2,320	PRDB overcast	1,000
	3,000		3,000
		Corrected balance	2,320

If the purchases returns day book was overcast then the amount posted to the purchases ledger control account on the debit side for returns was £1,000 too big

and therefore an additional credit entry for £1,000 is needed in the control account.

The discount received of £680 were omitted from the control account therefore the control account must be debited with this amount.

Step 5

- correct any errors that affect the total of the list of balances from the subsidiary (purchases) ledger
- find corrected total of list of subsidiary (purchases) ledger balances.

	£
Total list of balances	2,500
Less: transposition error on invoice (530 – 350)	(180)
Corrected total list of balances	2,320

The invoice had been entered as £180 higher than it should have been and therefore the total of the list of balances must be reduced by £180.

Example

Sales ledger control account reconciliation

	£
Balance per sales ledger control account	4,580
Total of list of subsidiary (sales) ledger balances	4,780
Difference	200

In this case the list of balances is £200 higher than the control account total. What may have caused this?

Suppose that one balance in the list of balances is for £100. It is possible that this is in fact a credit balance of £100 but has been incorrectly added into the list of balances rather than being deducted.

Alternatively, if the control account includes an irrecoverable debt write off of £200, then it is possible that this has not been entered into the individual account in the subsidiary (sales) ledger, causing the subsidiary (sales) ledger balances to be higher than the control account balance.

VAT control accounts

As seen in Bookkeeping Transactions, as the sales, sales returns, purchases and purchases returns are entered into the accounts, the VAT is also calculated and accounted for.

Within the BKCL assessment you may be given extracts from the day books and asked to enter the relevant figures into the VAT control account, or you may be asked to list the entries required to the control account indicating whether they would be on the debit or credit side of the VAT control account.

It may also be a requirement to find the overall balance of the VAT control account i.e. to state what the balance is and whether it is owed to the tax authorities (HMRC) or whether a refund is due from them. The illustration above has shown us the VAT control account assuming that the balance brought down is on the credit side and therefore a liability. Although it is less likely, you may also encounter a VAT control account where the balance brought down is on the debit side and therefore an asset, meaning a refund is due to the business from the tax authorities.

VAT control account

	£		£
VAT on credit purchases		VAT on credit sales	
VAT on cash purchases		VAT on cash sales	
VAT on sales returns		VAT on purchases returns	
Balance c/d			
	_____		_____
	_____		_____
		Balance b/d	

10

Payroll procedures

- Gross pay and deductions.
- Total wages cost.
- Paying wages and salaries.
- Accounting for wages and salaries.
- Paying PAYE and NIC.

Gross pay and deductions

Gross pay

Made up of:

Basic wage + overtime + bonus + shift payment + commission etc

Net pay

	£
Gross pay	X
Less: PAYE	(X)
Less: Employee's NIC	(X)
Less: other deductions	(X)
Net pay to employee	X

PAYE

- deduction of income tax due on gross pay
- employer deducts correct amount of income tax for period from gross pay
- employer pays this income tax to HM Revenue and Customs (HMRC).

National Insurance Contributions (NIC)

- two types – employee's NIC
- – employer's NIC
- employee's NIC – deducted from gross pay by employer
- – paid over to HMRC by employer
- employer's NIC – additional payment to HMRC by employer.

Other possible deductions

- pension contributions
- payments under save as you earn scheme (SAYE)
- payments under give as you earn scheme (GAYE)
- others such as subscriptions to sports/ social clubs, trade unions.

Total wages cost

Cost to employer = Gross pay + employer's NIC + employer's pension contributions

Paying wages and salaries

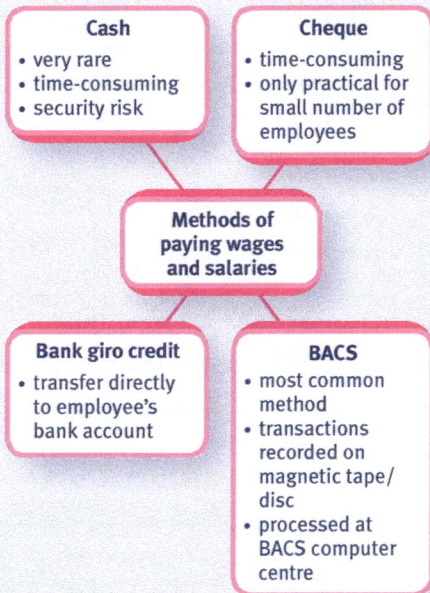

Cash
- very rare
- time-consuming
- security risk

Cheque
- time-consuming
- only practical for small number of employees

Methods of paying wages and salaries

Bank giro credit
- transfer directly to employee's bank account

BACS
- most common method
- transactions recorded on magnetic tape/ disc
- processed at BACS computer centre

Example

Gross pay of employee = £500 per week
PAYE   = £100 for week
Employee's NIC   = £80 for week
Employer's NIC   = £90 for week

	£	
Gross pay	500	
Less: PAYE	(100)	Paid by employer to HMRC
Less: Employee's NIC	(80)	Paid by employer to HMRC
Employee's net pay	320	Paid to employee

Employer pays:

	£
Net pay to employee	320
PAYE to HMRC	100
Employee's NIC to HMRC	80
Employer's NIC to HMRC	90
Total cost to employer	590

Total wages cost to employer:

	£
Gross pay	500
Employer's NIC	90
	590

Accounting for wages and salaries

e.g

Double entry – two fundamentals

Cost to employer = gross pay + employer's NIC + employer's pension contributions

PAYE and NIC deductions paid over to HMRC by employer

The wages and salaries control account is used to ensure that all wages and salaries costs are correctly paid out to the appropriate parties

Example

Double entry

Gross pay of employee	= £500 per week
PAYE	= £100 for week
Employee's NIC	= £80 for week
Employer's NIC	= £90 for week

Step 1 – Gross pay

Debit Wages expense account £590
Credit Wages and salaries control £590
      account

Wages expense account

	£		£
Wages and salaries control	590		

Wages and salaries control account

	£		£
		Wages expense	590

Step 2 – net pay

| Debit | Wages and salaries control account (£500 – £100 – £80) | £320 |
| Credit | Bank account | £320 |

Wages expense account

	£		£
Wages and salaries control	590		

Wages and salaries control account

	£		£
Bank	320	Wages expense	590

Step 3 – deductions payable to HMRC

| Debit | Wages and salaries control account (£100 + £80 + £90) | £270 |
| Credit | PAYE/NIC account | £270 |

Wages expense account

	£		£
Wages and salaries control	590		

Wages and salaries control account

	£		£
Bank	320	Wages expense	590
PAYE/NIC	270		

PAYE/NIC account

	£		£
		Wages and salaries control	270

Overall result – balance accounts

Wages expense account

	£		£
Wages and salaries control	590		
		balance c/d	590
	590		590
balance b/d	590		

= total wages cost for period (debit balance = expense)

Wages and salaries control account

	£		£
Bank	320	Wages expense	590
PAYE/NIC	270		
	590		590

= no balance – simply a control account.

PAYE/NIC

	£		£
Balance c/d	270	Wages and salaries control	270
	270		270
		Balance b/d	270

= amount due to HMRC
(credit balance = liability).

Paying PAYE and NIC

- payment of amounts deducted and due for PAYE, employee's and employer's NIC made each month

- made by bank giro credit to HM Revenue and Customs

- one payment covering all employees.

Double entry

Debit	PAYE/NIC account
Credit	Bank account

PAYE/NIC account

	£		£
		Wages and salaries control	270
Balance c/d	270		
	270		270
Bank	270	Balance b/d	270

11

Bank reconciliations

- Calculating the balance on the cash book.
- Comparing the cash book and the bank statement.
- Bank reconciliation statement.

Calculating the balance on the cash book

If a separate cash receipts book and cash payments book are used then the balance on the cash book at the end of the period is:

Balance on cash book	=	Opening cash book balance	+	Cash book receipts total	−	Cash book payments total

e.g

Example

A business had a balance on its cash book at 1 May of £750 debit. During May the cash receipts book shows a total of £5,340 and the cash payments book shows a total of £5,720.

Balance on cash book at end of May
= £750 + £5,340 − £5,720
= £370

Example

A business had a balance on its cash book at 1 May of £750 but this time it was a credit balance or overdraft balance. During May the cash receipts book shows a total of £5,340 and the cash payments book shows a total of £5,720.

Balance on cash book at end of May
= -£750 + £5,340 - £5,720
= £1,130 overdraft

Comparing the cash book and the bank statement

When the bank statement is received it should be checked to the cash book to ensure the accuracy of the cash book.

Debits and credits on bank statement

- a debit on the bank statement is a payment
- a credit on the bank statement is a deposit
- this is the opposite way round to the business ledger account as the bank statement is prepared from the bank's point of view.

Procedure

Step 1

- tick off items found in both cash book and on bank statement.

Step 2

- consider the unticked items in cash book and bank statement.

Unticked items in cash book

Items in cash book but not on bank statement

Outstanding lodgements
Cheques paid into bank but not on bank statement yet

Unpresented cheques
Cheques written by business but not cleared onto bank statement

Errors in cash book which cannot be matched to bank statement

Unticked items on bank statement

Direct debits/ standing orders

payments made directly out of the bank which have not been entered into cash payments book

Direct credits/ BACS receipts

credits directly into the bank account which have not yet been entered into cash receipts book

Items on bank statement but not in cash book

Bank charges/ interest

not yet in cash book as cashier does not know about them until bank statement received

Errors in cash book

errors such as transposition errors which only come to light when cash book is compared to bank statement

Bank reconciliation statement

Step 1 Compare cash book to bank statement

- covered above.

Step 2 Enter items which are on bank statement but not yet in cash book into the cash book

- typical items include bank charges, direct debits, direct credits or standing orders

- correct any errors in the cash book.

Step 3 Balance amended cash book

- this should give the correct balance on the cash book

- this will not usually agree with the bank statement balance due to timing differences.

Step 4 Prepare bank reconciliation statement

Bank reconciliation statement

	£
Balance per bank statement	X
Less: unpresented cheques	(X)
Add: outstanding lodgements	X
Balance per cash book	X

Once the unpresented cheques and outstanding lodgements have been taken into account the bank statement balance should agree to the amended cash book balance. The cash book and bank statement are reconciled.

Example

A company's cashier has compared the cash book for the month of May to the bank statement at 31 May. The following differences have been noted:

- bank charges of £35 on the bank statement not in cash book
- direct debit of £100 on bank statement not in cash book
- cheques written by the business totalling £340 not yet on bank statement
- cheques paid into bank account totalling £200 not yet on bank statement.

The balance on the cash book before this reconciliation took place was a debit balance of £700 but the balance on the bank statement was £705 in credit.

Amend cash book

Cash book

	£		£
Original balance	700	Bank charges	35
		Direct debit	100
		Amended closing balance	565
	700		700
Amended cash book balance	565		

Prepare bank reconciliation statement

	£
Balance per bank statement	705
Less: unpresented cheques	(340)
Add: outstanding lodgements	200
Balance per cash book	565

12

Materials and inventory

- Different types of inventory.
- Valuing raw materials.
- Valuing WIP and finished goods.
- Calculating an overhead cost per unit.

Different types of inventory

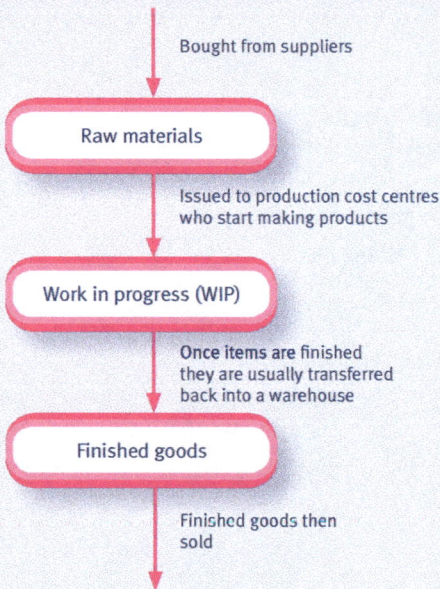

Bought from suppliers

Raw materials

Issued to production cost centres who start making products

Work in progress (WIP)

Once items are finished they are usually transferred back into a warehouse

Finished goods

Finished goods then sold

Valuing raw materials

Need to value issues of inventory and closing inventory

	True	False
LIFO costs issues of inventory at the most recent purchase price.	✓	
FIFO costs issues of inventory at the oldest purchase price.	✓	
AVCO costs issues of inventory at an average purchase price.	✓	
LIFO values closing inventory at the oldest purchase price.	✓	
In times of increasing prices LIFO will give a lower profit figure than FIFO and AVCO.	✓	
FIFO values closing inventory at the most recent purchase price.	✓	
In times of increasing prices FIFO will give a higher profit figure than LIFO or AVCO.	✓	
AVCO values closing inventory at an average purchase price.	✓	

Example

Swall Ltd has the following movements in a certain type of inventory into and out of it stores for the month of May:

Date	Receipts			Issues	
	Kg	Price / Kg	Cost	Kg	Cost
May 1	200	£4.50	£900		
May 2	100	£5.40	£540		
May 3				50	

Complete the table below for the issue and closing inventory values.

Method	Cost of issue	Closing inventory
FIFO		
LIFO		
AVCO		

Solution

Method	Cost of issue	Closing inventory
FIFO	£225	£1,215
LIFO	£270	£1,170
AVCO	£240	£1,200

Workings

FIFO

- The 50kg issued on the 3rd May will all come from the earliest purchase made on the 1st May.
- Thus the cost of the issue will be 50kg@£4.50 = £225
- Total purchases = £1,440, so closing inventory = 1,440 − 225 = £1,215

LIFO

- The 50kg issued on the 3rd May will all come from the most recent purchase made on the 2nd May.
- Thus the cost of the issue will be 50kg@£5.40 = £270
- Closing inventory = 1,440 − 270 = £1,170

AVCO

- We bought 300kg at a total cost of 900 + 540 = £1,440
- On average this works out at 1,440/300 = £4.80/kg
- Thus the cost of the issue will be 50kg@£4.80 = £240
- Closing inventory = 1,440 − 240 = £1,200

Valuing WIP and finished goods

Example cost card

The cost per unit for completed goods could show the following:

	Cost/unit £
Direct labour cost (2 hours @£10/hour)	20
Direct material cost	3
Direct expenses	1
Prime cost	24
Production overheads (2 hours @ £4/hour)	8
Total cost per unit	32

Direct costs

- Direct materials could be identified using job cards and information on stores requisitions.
- Direct labour can be identified using job cards and time sheets.

Indirect costs

- Unit basis – each unit gets the same level of overhead.
- Labour rate basis.

Calculating an overhead cost per unit

There are 3 approaches that you need to be familiar with for this assessment for calculating an overhead cost per unit. The 3 absorption bases are:

- A rate per machine hour
- A rate per labour hour
- A rate per unit

Example

Total factory activity for Johnstone Ltd is forecast as follows:

Machine hours	10,000
Labour hours	12,500
No. of units	60,000
Overheads	£150,000

Absorption rates can be calculated using the 3 bases as follows:

	Machine hour	Labour hour	Unit
Overheads (£)	150,000	150,000	150,000
Activity	10,000	12,500	60,000
Absorption rate	15.00	12.00	2.50

Factory cost of goods sold

	£
Opening inventory of raw materials	7,000
Purchases of raw materials	50,000
Closing inventory of raw materials	(10,000)
Direct materials used	47,000
Direct labour	97,000
Direct cost	**144,000**
Manufacturing overheads	53,000
Manufacturing cost	**197,000**
Opening inventory of work in progress	8,000
Closing inventory of work in progress	(10,000)
Cost of goods manufactured	**195,000**
Opening inventory of finished goods	30,000
Closing inventory of finished goods	(25,000)
Cost of goods sold	**200,000**

13

Labour costs

- Time related pay.
- Output related pay.
- Bonus schemes.

Time related pay

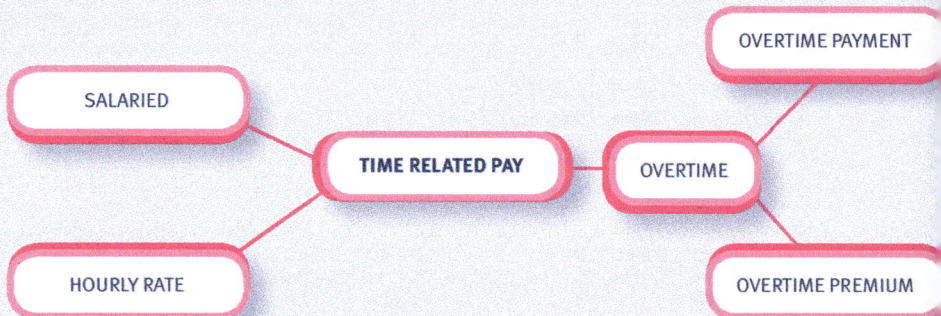

Output related pay

```
┌──────────────────┐     ┌──────────────┐     ┌──────────────────┐
│  PAID FIXED      │     │   OUTPUT     │     │  GUARANTEED      │
│  AMOUNT PER      │─────│   RELATED    │─────│  MINIMUM         │
│  UNIT OF         │     │   PAY        │     │  PAYMENT         │
│  OUTPUT          │     │              │     │                  │
└──────────────────┘     └──────────────┘     └──────────────────┘
```

Bonus schemes

Payment method	Time-rate	Piece rate	Time-rate plus bonus
Labour is paid according to hours worked.	✓		
Labour is paid based on the production achieved.		✓	
Labour is paid extra if an agreed level of output is exceeded.			✓

Payment method	Time-rate	Piece rate	Time-rate plus bonus
Assured level of remuneration for employee.	✓		
Employee earns more if they work more efficiently than expected.		✓	
Assured level of remuneration and reward for working efficiently.			✓

14

Budgeting

- Budgeting.
- Variances.

Budgeting

What is budgeting?

Budgets set out the costs and revenues that are expected to be incurred or earned in future periods.

Most organisations prepare budgets for the business as a whole. The following budgets may also be prepared by organisations:

- Departmental budgets.
- Functional budgets (for sales, production, expenditure and so on).
- Income statements (in order to determine the expected future profits).
- Cash budgets (in order to determine future cash flows).

Budgetary control

The main reason for budgeting is to help managers control the business.

The budget gives a benchmark against which we can evaluate actual performance.

Any difference or variance can then be investigated to identify the cause. Once we know this we can take appropriate action.

Variances

| Variance | = | difference between actual figure and comparison figure. |

| Favourable variance | = | actual result better than comparison figure. |

| Adverse variance | = | actual results worse than comparison figure. |

Note: here the comparison figure will be the budget.

Example

Cost type	Budget £	Actual £	Variance £	Adv.	Fav.
Materials	24,500	26,200	1,700	✓	

Evaluating the significance of a variance

Management do not want to waste time investigating small variances, so will set criteria for deciding what makes a variance large enough to report and investigate.

For example,

- 'Only investigate variances bigger than £500'.
- 'Only investigate variances bigger that 5% of budget'.

If using a percentage measure then the amount of the variance that exceeds the cut-off percentage is known as the 'discrepancy'.

Reporting variances

It stands to reason that variances should be reported to the individual responsible for them happening, or who can take action on them.

For example, a Direct Materials cost variance that is due to materials price paid – report to Purchasing Manager.

Sales variance – report to Sales Manager.

15

The role of the finance function

- Introduction.
- Key aspects of accounting and solvency.
- Policies and procedures within the finance function.

Introduction

The work of accountants

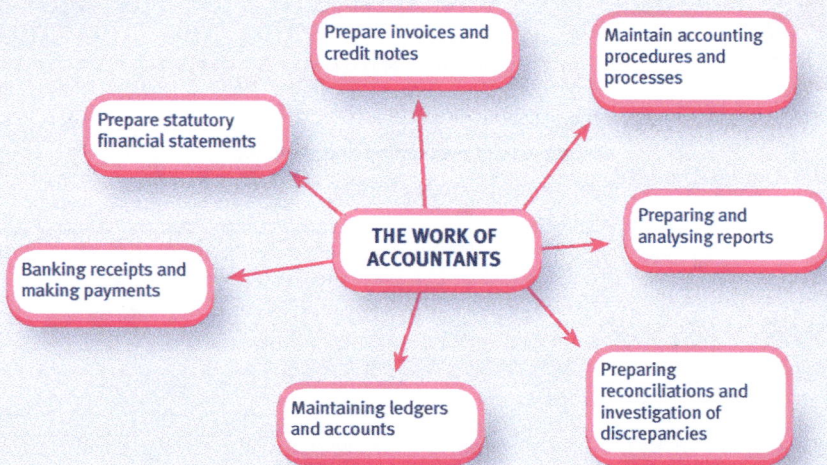

Key aspects of accounting and solvency

Financial accounting and management accounting

Financial accounting	Management accounting
Limited companies are required by law to prepare annual financial statements	Records are not mandatory
The cost of record-keeping is a necessity	The cost of record-keeping needs to be justified
Objectives and uses are not defined by management	Objectives and uses are decided by management
Mainly a historical record	Concerned with future results as well as historical data
Information must be compiled prudently and in accordance with legal and accounting requirements	Information should be compiled as management requires – the key criterion being relevance
Prepared for external reporting	Prepared for internal use only

Types of information

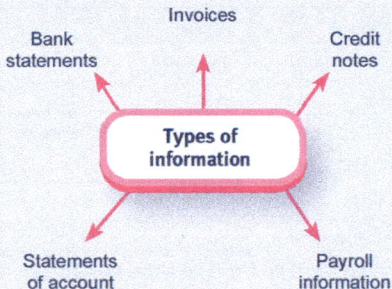

Invoices

Bank statements

Credit notes

Types of information

Statements of account

Payroll information

Note – for information to be useful, it must be **complete, timely, accurate and fit for purpose.**

Solvency

Solvency is the financial soundness of an organisation that allows it to discharge its monetary obligations (such as paying payables on time) as they fall due. To this end they must ensure that they have cash available to meet these obligations.

Ways to manage or improve solvency

- regular reconciliation of bank balances to highlight bank charges and interest, direct debit and standing order payments and BACS receipts from customers to monitor transactions passing through the bank account

- awareness of bank account balances to identify whether they may become overdrawn and to plan ways to avoid the overdraft or incur the changes and interest

- awareness of how much is owed to the organisation by maintaining a sales ledger control account
- awareness of how much is owed by the organisation by maintaining a purchase ledger control account, and other records such as loan liabilities and recognising when they are due for payment
- awareness and use of forward planning to identify whether there is a need to arrange for increased or extended credit or loan facilities to meet organisation needs
- awareness and use of forward planning to identify whether it is advantageous, and on what terms, to offer credit facilities and discounts to customers and whether it is beneficial to use credit facilities and discounts offered by suppliers.

Policies and procedures within the finance function

Legal obligations

Legal obligations
- Statutory financial statements
- VAT returns and payment dates
- Corporation tax
- Data protection
- Health and safety

Internal policies

16

Comparison and communication of information

- Comparison of information.
- Communication of information.

Comparison of information

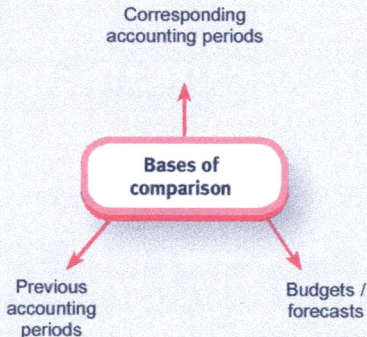

Corresponding accounting periods

↑

Bases of comparison

↙   ↘

Previous accounting periods   Budgets / forecasts

Definition

Variance analysis is the quantification of differences between what was expected and what actually occurred, followed by investigation of what caused the differences and implementation of appropriate corrective action.

Variances may be expressed either as monetary amounts or as a percentage of the expected or budgeted amount.

Variances may **be favourable** where income is greater than expected, or when costs are less than expected. Variances may be **adverse** where income is less than expected or costs are greater then expected.

A specimen variance report may look as follows:

Costs – week 17	Budget £	Actual £	Variance £
Material X	117,000	120,000	3,000 adverse
Material Y	270,000	250,000	20,000 favourable
Labour	226,000	230,000	4,000 adverse

You may be presented with actual costs and need to calculate the budgeted figures before you can complete the variance report. Note that the variances could also be presented as a percentage of the budgeted figure, rather than as a monetary amount.

Investigation of variances is normally limited to those which are regarded as significant. Whether a variance is regarded as significant or not is normally dependent upon the variance exceeding either a specified monetary amount e.g. £3,000 or a predefined percentage e.g. a significant variance is one that differs from the budgeted figure by more than 5%.

Communication of information

Communication of information should be made in a timely, appropriate and professional manner. For example, any report, memorandum or email should be formatted and presented, perhaps with the use of headings, paragraphs and bullet points to provide structure. Professional business language should be used at all times.

Remember to consider confidentiality of information – do you have approval from a responsible person (e.g. your manager) to communicate information to another person (e.g. a supplier or the sales director) particularly if that information could be regarded as being personal or sensitive in any way?

17

Planning and organising work

- Organisation charts.
- Authority, responsibility and delegation.
- Organisational objectives.
- Work planning – routines.
- Work planning – relevant issues.
- Work planning – methods.
- Work planning – difficulties.

Organisation charts

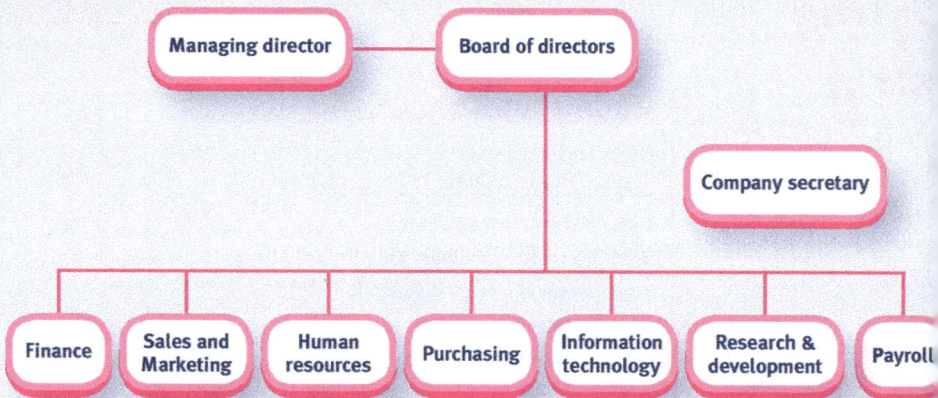

```
        ┌──────────────────┐        ┌──────────────────┐
        │ Managing director│────────│ Board of directors│
        └──────────────────┘        └──────────────────┘
                                              │
                                              │      ┌──────────────────┐
                                              │      │ Company secretary│
                                              │      └──────────────────┘
                                              │
   ┌──────┬──────────┬──────────┬────────────┼──────────┬──────────────┬────────┐
┌───────┐┌──────────┐┌──────────┐┌──────────┐┌───────────┐┌──────────────┐┌────────┐
│Finance││ Sales and││  Human   ││Purchasing││Information ││  Research &  ││ Payroll│
│       ││ Marketing││ resources││          ││ technology ││  development  ││        │
└───────┘└──────────┘└──────────┘└──────────┘└───────────┘└──────────────┘└────────┘
```

Organisation charts help individuals to understand the structure of an organisation and they are often prepared on a hierarchal basis. Similar charts can be prepared on a departmental basis, e.g. finance department, or on a sectional basis e.g. financial and management accounting sections within the finance department.

Authority, responsibility and delegation

Definition

Authority is defined as the right that an individual has to direct certain actions of others i.e. it is the right to use power.

Responsibility is defined as the duty of an official to carry out his or her assigned task or to ensure it is completed.

Delegation is defined as the act by which a person transfers part of their authority to a subordinate person.

Organisational objectives

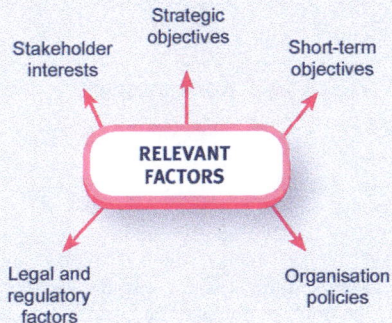

Stakeholder interests

Strategic objectives

Short-term objectives

RELEVANT FACTORS

Legal and regulatory factors

Organisation policies

Work planning – routines

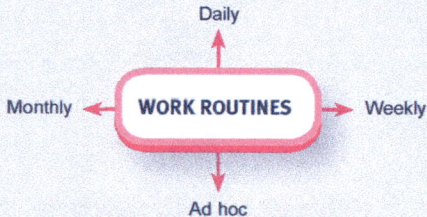

For shorter-term planning, this may involve scheduling activities within the week or day ahead. They may need to be reorganised depending upon the needs of the business, including dealing with ad hoc activities that may arise.

Work planning – relevant issues

Planning requires not only identification of the tasks or duties to be performed within a given timescale, but also an estimate of the time each item will take. For longer-term planning, this will help to identify potential problems, and enable rescheduling of activities so that they can be achieved within required timescales.

Work planning – methods

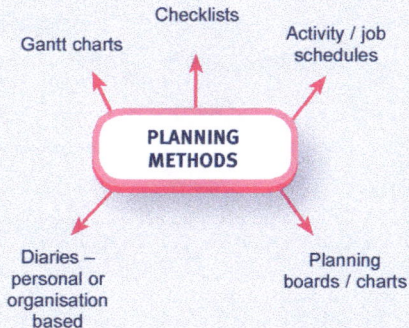

Checklists

Gantt charts

Activity / job schedules

PLANNING METHODS

Diaries – personal or organisation based

Planning boards / charts

Work planning – difficulties

One important point about planning is that it helps to identify potential problems before they arise. Potential problems can then be reported to an appropriate person so that action may be taken to avoid or minimise the problem. For example, bottlenecks and clashes of commitments can be identified and amended to remove the problem.

Problems may be unexpected, such as system crashes or a colleague absent due to illness. In these situations, current plans need to be reconsidered and amended, which may include amending priorities.

Working relationships

- Introduction.
- Methods of communication.
- Confidential information.
- Interpersonal skills.
- Teams.
- Handling disagreements and conflicts.

Introduction

Working relationships require co-ordination, communication and co-operation to achieve individual and organisational objectives.

Effective organisations are dependent upon effective communication, both within the organisation, and with outside third parties.

One important relationship is the contractual relationship between an employer and its employees. An employee has the following duties to their employer:

- a duty of care to perform their work with reasonable care
- a duty of co-operation to achieve their employers' legitimate objectives
- a duty of obedience to comply will all legal and reasonable instructions
- a duty of loyal service not to have any competing or conflicting interests with their employer.

Note that an employee cannot be forced to break the law, such as being told to exceed the speed limit to deliver goods to a customer by a specified time.

The contractual relationship between employee and employer (and between employees) is also underpinned by other relevant legislation.

Equal opportunities legislation

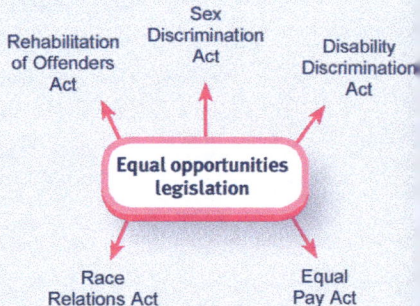

Rehabilitation of Offenders Act

Sex Discrimination Act

Disability Discrimination Act

Equal opportunities legislation

Race Relations Act

Equal Pay Act

Note that other laws, such as the National Minimum Wage Act are also relevant to the employer-employee relationship.

Methods of communication

Whichever method of business communication is used, it must be in an appropriate manner – professional, courteous and informative. It is important to use an appropriate method of communication e.g. is it a brief, informal verbal exchange of information between colleagues who work next to each other, or is it a formal communication containing lots of fact and technical detail best conveyed in a written document?

Remember that, with any form of communication, if it is not professional, courteous and informative, this may result in problems between colleagues or with external parties such as suppliers or customers.

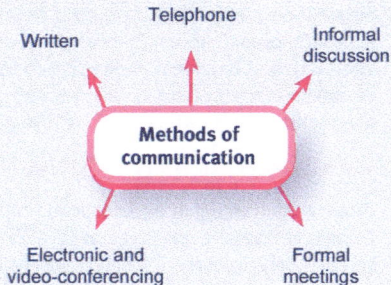

Written   Telephone   Informal discussion

Methods of communication

Electronic and video-conferencing   Formal meetings

Effective communication is timely, accurate and appropriate. Ensure that you review written communication before it is despatched. You should plan in advance for any meetings you are due to attend by considering things you intend to comment upon (or indeed, information that you don't want to communicate).

Ensure that any information is appropriately addressed or directed so that it reaches only the intended recipient(s) and does not result in breach or loss of confidential or sensitive information. It is almost impossible to retract or cancel inappropriate or misdirected communication, in whatever form it may take.

Confidential information

Employees working in an accounting and finance function usually have access to confidential information. Caution should be exercised when dealing with information that may be regarded as confidential that it is not used or disclosed in an inappropriate manner.

Maintaining confidentiality of information may apply to not disclosing information to others in the organisation, such as not disclosing salary and personal contact details of individual employees to colleagues. Maintaining confidentiality of information also applies to not disclosing information to others outside of the organisation, such as disclosing the bank account details of the organisation to anyone not authorised to receive them.

Equally, third parties, such as suppliers, who provide confidential or sensitive information to you or your organisation for business purposes have the right to expect that it will be treated appropriately and not disclosed without appropriate authority.

Many organisations apply controls and procedures to reduce the risk of accidental or deliberate disclosure of confidential information by employees. Examples of controls and procedures include:

- restricted access to confidential information

- authorisation and approval procedures t access confidential information

- clear communication of organisational policy on managing confidential and sensitive information

- employee training and awareness of what is expected of those with access to confidential and sensitive information.

Organisations also need to be aware of the risk of others hacking into their information systems to gain access to confidential or sensitive information. This risk may be mitigated by operating effective IT controls such as firewalls, maintaining logs of attempted unauthorised access to data and following up on such instances.

The law relating to data protection and copyright is considered elsewhere in this publication. In addition, ethical responsibilities relating to confidentiality are also considered elsewhere in this publication.

Unauthorised disclosure of confidential information may lead to problems such as:

- embarrassment for those involved
- loss of reputation

- legal proceedings, leading to fines, penalties or compensation awards
- professional disciplinary proceedings.

Interpersonal skills

Definition

Interpersonal skills – the interactive, face-to-face or social skills used to establish and maintain relationships between people.

Improving interpersonal skills

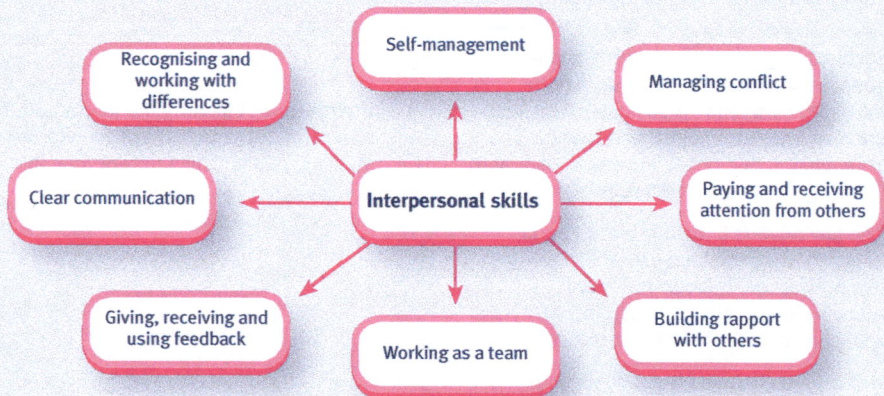

Teams

Very few individuals work in isolation to others, people invariably work in teams. A team may be a permanent arrangement, such as the purchase ledger team in an organisation, or it may be set up to achieve a particular purpose or project, such as implementation of a new IT system, and then disbanded. Teams usually consist of individuals with diverse personalities, skill sets and experiences. They do, however, share common goals or objectives. To achieve those objectives, mutual communication and understanding is required.

Features of effective teamwork

- Clearly defined goals or objectives for the team to achieve or complete
- Clearly defined joint or individual responsibilities

- Team members involved in goal setting or timescales/methods to achieve completion
- Team members possess a range of competences, skills and technical knowledge
- Commitment to achieve the team, joint and individual objectives
- Mutual trust and support of team members
- Effective communication between team members.

Handling disagreements and conflicts

Managing disagreement requires honest and open communication between the relevant parties, often with a supervisor or manager to mediate or oversee the process.

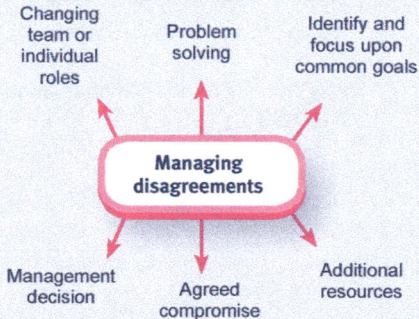

Critical factors in successful negotiation to manage disagreement and conflict are as follows:

- entitlement to ask questions
- responsibility to listen to others
- willingness to empathise with others
- mutual respect
- trust and honesty.

Any negotiator or mediator managing disagreements needs certain skills: **interpersonal, analytical and technical**. Ideally, both parties should feel that they have benefited from the negotiation or mediation process and have obtained or gained something from the process, a 'win-win' outcome.

If good working relationships are maintained morale, motivation and commitment is improved, along with employees willing to be supportive of each other, leading to improved efficiency and productivity.

19

Policies, procedures and legislation

- Risks to data.
- Protecting data from risks.
- Retention of documents.
- Data Protection Act.
- Patent and copyright law.
- Health and Safety at Work Act 1974.
- Internal policies and procedures.

Risks to data

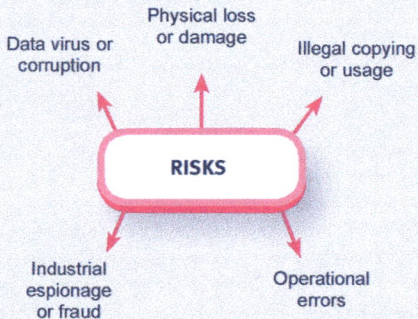

Data virus or corruption

Physical loss or damage

Illegal copying or usage

RISKS

Industrial espionage or fraud

Operational errors

Note that risks to data include loss or unauthorised disclosure to anyone who should not have access to it.

Protecting data from risks

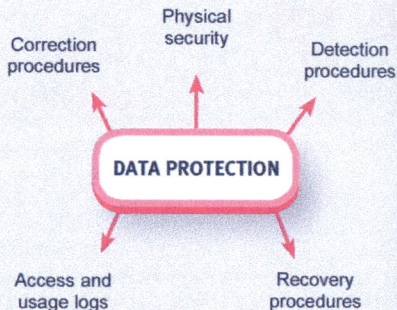

Correction procedures

Physical security

Detection procedures

DATA PROTECTION

Access and usage logs

Recovery procedures

This may also include policies and procedures to inform staff of the importance of data protection, including maintaining confidentiality of data where required.

Retention of documents

This is particularly important for employees working in an accounting department. There are legal requirements to retain accounting records for at least six years, whilst payroll data must be retained for three years.

Accounting records form the basis of information compiled for management accounting, decision-making and control purposes. They also form the basis of preparation of the financial statements provided to stakeholders and regulators, such as HM Revenue & Customs, upon which corporate tax and VAT liabilities are determined.

Data Protection Act

Underlying principles:

- Processed fairly and lawfully
- Obtained for specified and lawful purposes
- Adequate, relevant and not excessive
- Accurate and up-to-date
- Retained no longer than necessary
- Processed in accordance with 'data subject's' rights
- Securely maintained
- Not transferred to any other country without equivalent data protection safeguards in place.

Any 'data subject' who has data held by an organisation has the right to receive details of **what information** is held about them, **why it is being held** and **who that information may be disclosed to.**

Patent and copyright law

This is law dealing with intellectual property such as sound recordings, film and television broadcasts, books and publications and computer programmes and software.

The law gives the creator or owner of intellectual property the right to use, sell, publish, reproduce or authorise third party use in exchange for a royalty. Unauthorised use of intellectual property may result in the unauthorised user being subject to legal action from the owner.

Health and Safety at Work Act 1974

Employer duties

Provide a safe working environment

Provide safe access to/from premises

Co-operation with H&SAW officials

Legal obligations

Provide safe equipment, training, operating and supervision

Investigation of accidents

Employee duties

Legal obligations

- Co-operate with H&S officials
- Not to misuse equipment
- Responsibility for own H&S
- Awareness and compliance with H&S policies
- Use equipment safely per training and guidance

Internal policies and procedures

These help to ensure that an organisation is aware of, and complies with, relevant laws and regulations. They also help employees to understand their rights, entitlements, duties and responsibilities. They are often available in a staff handbook, which may be in either hardcopy or softcopy form.

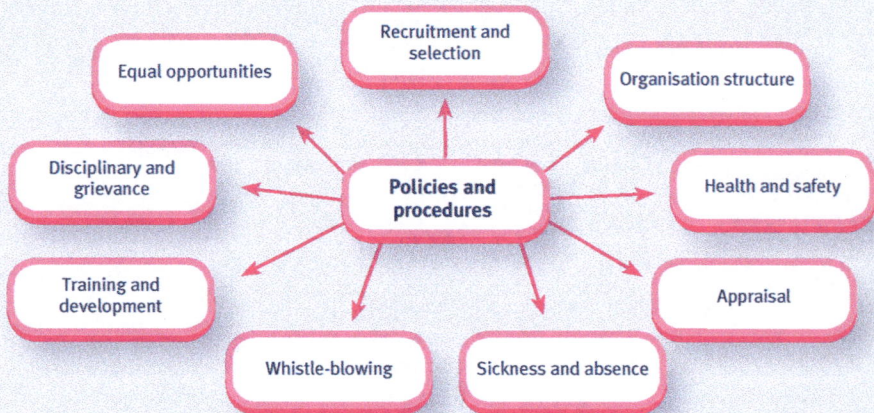

20

Improving your own performance

- Development needs and activities.
- Career planning.
- Review and evaluation of performance.

Development needs and activities

Definition

Development – the growth or realisation of a person's ability and potential, through the provision of learning and educational experiences.

Continuing Professional Development ('CPD') – the process of maintaining and developing your professional skills throughout your career. It covers any learning activity that is relevant to your current or future career.

Development activities

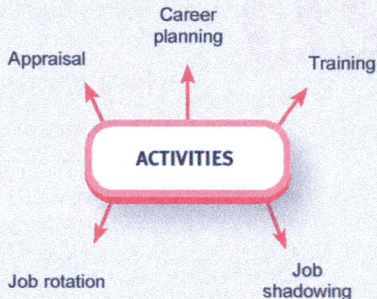

ACTIVITIES

Appraisal

Career planning

Training

Job rotation

Job shadowing

CPD activities

- 'Soft skills' courses
- Professional qualifications
- Conferences
- Technical courses
- **ACTIVITIES**
- Job shadowing or secondments
- Technical & professional literature
- Appraisal feedback and outcomes

Career planning

Definition

SWOT analysis – A framework for analysing personal Strengths, Weaknesses, Opportunities and Threats as a basis for helping to determine career plans.

One way of developing an understanding of career aspirations and goals is to perform a SWOT analysis, with relevant considerations identified for each element of analysis.

Strengths	Weaknesses
What are your capabilities?	What could you improve upon?
What do you do well?	What do you do less well?
	What work-related activities do you dislike?
Opportunities	**Threats**
Is there staff turnover to provide opportunity to change job?	What obstacles do you face?
What are the current work-related trends or requirements?	Are others better qualified or more competent in their work?

A related activity to assist career planning is to perform a competence assessment.

Definition

Competence assessment – An assessment of how well or otherwise an individual is performing the required job skills in comparison with specified performance standards.

Competences – The critical skills, knowledge and attitude required for a jobholder to perform effectively. Competences may be behavioural, occupational or generic.

Review and evaluation of performance

Review may take place in a number of ways

- practical – i.e. observation of person performing work activities

  - Written – i.e. a log or record of experience is compiled. This may be subject to review and approval by a manager

  - Oral – i.e. explaining to another person what you are doing, how it should be done and why it is done.

Methods of assessment of performance may be done:

- by grading as a pass/fail

  - by confirming that a person is competent/not yet competent at a task or activity

  - by identifying that there is not yet sufficient evidence upon which to assess performance.

21

Ethics and sustainability

- Ethical principles.
- Threats to ethical principles.
- Sustainability and corporate social responsibility.

Ethical principles

Definition

Ethics – a set of moral principles that governs the behaviour of individuals.

Professional competence and due care

Confidentiality

Objectivity

Ethical principles

Professional behaviour

Integrity

Confidentiality

Do not disclose information to third parties unless you have proper authority to do so, that you have a legal or professional right or duty to disclose information.

Do not use information acquired as a result of your business or work activities for personal advantage, or pass on that information for others to gain a personal advantage.

This will include non-disclosure of information to others within your organisatio e.g. not disclosing personal salary or contac details of a colleague to a co-worker.

Objectivity

All work activities should be undertaken without bias or conflict of interest so that the can be relied upon by others.

Professional competence and due care

Professional competence relates to having the underlying knowledge, skills and capabilities to perform your job. Due care relates to the application of knowledge, skills and capabilities when performing work.

If you fail to exercise due care in the performance of your work, potentially you will be regarded as being negligent.

Integrity

This relates to honesty and being straightforward in your dealings with others in the course of your work.

Professional behaviour

You should behave in such a way as to not bring disrepute upon yourself or your profession.

Threats to ethical principles

Self-interest

Objectivity may be threatened if your work or decision-making is compromised by having a personal interest in a transaction or event e.g. behaving in a way to give yourself or a friend or colleague a personal or financial benefit in a transaction or event.

Self-review

Objectivity may be compromised if you need to reconsider or review the results of your earlier work. You should not try to disguise or avoid making disclosure of errors or omissions in your work.

Advocacy

You should perform your work with an independent and objective manner, presenting information fully and in an impartial manner. Ideally, you should present full information and explanation to others so that they can make appropriate decisions.

If you are required to express a point of view or opinion on an issue, you should ensure that it is fully supported by factual information and that you present a balanced perspective, such as including references to possible risks or disadvantages of a particular course of action.

Familiarity

Objectivity may be compromised if you have undue familiarity with a situation or with the individuals involved. For example, you have been asked to investigate a particular transaction which appears to be unusual. Undue familiarity may be a problem if the colleague responsible for the transaction is a personal friend, or if you place too much reliance upon explanation and comment received, without proper consideration of what you have been told.

Intimidation

This risk to ethical behaviour may take several forms, such as financial intimidation by a customer threatening not to purchase goods from your organisation unless they are given preferential terms to which they are not entitled. It could also take the form of your manager requiring you to prepare information in a specified way that omits or disguises important details with the threat that, if you fail to comply, it may adversely affect your appraisal or salary grading. In rare cases, intimidation could be the threat of physical violence to you, family or colleagues.

Planning and foresight – if you become aware of any potential threats to ethical behaviour, you should advise your manager so that appropriate safeguards can be put in place to avoid or minimise any potential problem.

Similarly, it is not always possible to pre-empt all potential problems. If you become aware of an ethical problem that cannot be avoided, you should advise your manager so that appropriate action can be taken to minimise any potential problem.

Sustainability and corporate social responsibility

Sustainability – how to meet the needs of the present without compromising the ability of future generations to meet their own needs

Corporate Social Responsibility – defined as a business approach that contributes to sustainable development by delivering economic, social and environmental benefits for all stakeholders. This is often referred to as 'The Three P's' – People, Planet and Profit

The elements of 'People, Planet, and Profit' are inter-related. For example, upholding good ethical principles could apply to the relationships that people have in business, but could also relate to profit if upholding good ethical principles leads to increased profits over a period of time.

Note that implementing policies which promote sustainability may incur costs e.g. purchasing vehicles that are more fuel-efficient which may not necessarily be the lowest cost vehicle. However, many organisations now believe that socially responsible sustainability policies bring benefits, such as an enhanced business reputation along with improved employee morale and commitment. This, in turn, may lead to improved business efficiency and increased sales revenues from customers who share similar values.

CSR initiatives – people (CSR)

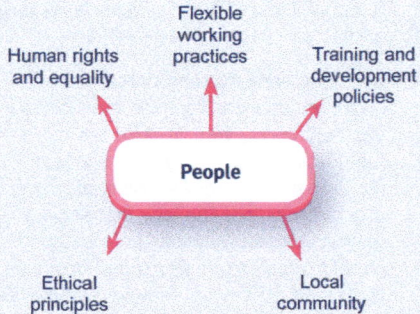

CSR initiatives – planet (environmental protection)

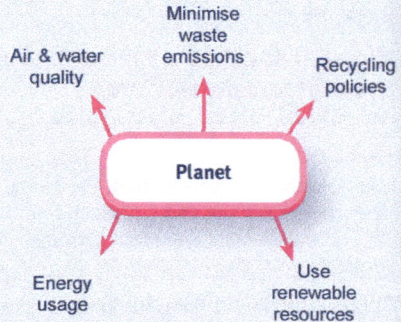

CSR initiatives – profit (business earnings)

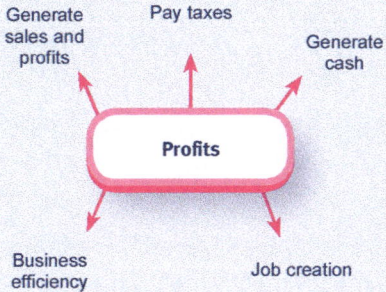

Generate sales and profits

Pay taxes

Generate cash

Profits

Business efficiency

Job creation

Index

A

Accounting equation 25, 26
Aged debt analysis 66
Analysed purchases day book 13
Analysed sales day book 10
Asset 25, 39, 91
Assigning responsibility for variances 152
Authorisation stamp 72
AVCO 140

B

BACS 125
BACS receipts 135
Bank charges 135
Bank giro credit 125
Bank reconciliation 131, 136, 137
Bank statement 134, 135
Bonus schemes 148
Books of prime entry 7
Budgetary control 150
Budgeting 150
Bulk discount 71

C

Capital 25
Capital expenditure 27
Capital income 27
Cash 32, 125
Cash book 78, 132, 134
Cash payments book 8, 17, 18, 77, 112
Cash receipts book 8, 15, 68, 70, 103, 104, 107
Casting error 92
Cheque 125
Compensation errors 92
Contra 96, 111
Contra entry 104, 105, 115
Credit 31, 34, 38, 39, 91
Credit note 57, 102
Credit notes 8, 11, 14, 72
Credit Purchases 45
Credit purchases returns 45
Credit sales 41
Credit sales returns 43

D

Debit 31, 38, 39, 91
Direct credits 135
Direct debit 135
Direct debits/standing orders 135
Discounts allowed 97, 104
Discounts received 112, 114
Double entry bookkeeping 31
Drawings 24
Dual effect 24

E

Employee's NIC 124
Employer's NIC 124
Errors 8, 92, 94, 96, 135
Errors of commission 92
Errors of omission 92
Errors of original entry 92
Errors of principle 92
Evaluating the significance of a variance 151
Expense 39, 91
Expenses 31
Extraction error 92

F

Factory cost of goods sold 144
FIFO 140
Finished goods 140

G

Give as you earn scheme (GAYE) 125
Goods received note/delivery note 71
Gross pay 124
Guaranteed minimum payment 147

I

Imprest system 80
Income 39, 91
Interest 135
Invoice 102, 112

J

Journal 8, 93

L

Ledger accounts 30, 31, 36
Ledger balances 38, 90
Liabilities 26

Liability 25, 39, 91
LIFO 140

N
National Insurance Contributions (NIC) 124
Net pay 124
Non-imprest system 80

O
Output related pay 147
Overtime payment 146
Overtime premium 146

P
Payables 25
PAYE 124, 130
Payments 65
Petty cash 85
Petty cash book 8, 21, 82, 83, 84, 85, 88
Petty cash box 80, 83, 88
Petty cash control account 86, 88
Petty cash control account reconciliation 88
Petty cash system 79
Petty cash vouchers 81

Purchase 13
Purchase day book 8, 12
Purchase invoices 8, 71
Purchase order 71
Purchases 58, 113
Purchases day book 12, 58, 59, 112, 113
Purchases ledger control account 58, 63, 112, 113, 114, 115, 116, 118, 119
Purchases ledger control account reconciliation 116, 117
Purchases returns 63, 113
Purchases returns day book 8, 14, 62, 112, 113

R
Raw materials 140
Receivable 25
Receivables' statements 66
Reconciling petty cash 86
Revenue expenditure 27
Revenue income 27

S

Sales 57
Sales day book 8, 9, 10, 51, 52, 102, 107
Sales invoice 8
Sales ledger control account 51, 53, 57, 102, 103, 104, 105, 107, 109, 110, 111, 115
Sales ledger control account reconciliation 107, 108, 120
Sales returns 57, 103
Sales returns day book 8, 11, 102, 103, 107
Save as you earn scheme (SAYE) 125
Separate entity 24
Single entry 92
Standing order 135
Subsidiary ledger 70
Subsidiary ledgers 49
Subsidiary (purchases) ledger 60, 61, 64, 77, 116, 118
Subsidiary (sales) ledger 53, 57, 107, 109, 110
Supplier's statements 74
Suspense account 94, 96, 97, 98, 99

T

Time related pay 146
Trade discount 71
Transposition error 92
Trial balance 38, 90

V

Valuing raw materials 140
Valuing WIP and finished goods 142
Variances 151
VAT 16

W

Wages and salaries 125, 127, 128
Work in progress (WIP) 140